The Old House Handbook for Chicago and Suburbs

This beautifully restored Lincoln Park Queen Anne is the kind of old house many of us dream of.

The
Old House Handbook
for Chicago and
Suburbs

ED SHARP

Chicago Review Press

Copyright © 1979 by Ed Sharp

First Edition

First Printing

Book design and typography by Claire J. Mahoney

ISBN (paperback edition) 0-914090-66-6

Library of Congress Catalog Number 79-64243

Published by
Chicago Review Press, Inc.
215 West Ohio Street
Chicago, Illinois 60610

Contents

CHAPTER 6

The Renovation — Preliminaries 97

CHAPTER 7

The Exterior Repair 125

CHAPTER 8

The Interior Renovation 141

Introduction

Old House Handbook is a guide to the entire renovation experience for people who are interested in buying an older building but need insight into what a renovation entails. *Old House Handbook* explains the financial complexities and the financial advantages of buying in an old city neighborhood. It describes how old neighborhoods regenerate and where in the Chicago area to look for an attractive old house or small multi-unit apartment building at a risk and a price you can afford. It tells you where to begin your renovation, what repairs to attempt yourself and what to leave to professionals. Perhaps most important of all, *Old House Handbook* gives you a "feel" for what buying and renovating a house in Chicago is all about.

Much of the information presented here is drawn from interviews with more than fifty people living in the Chicago area who either have renovated their own houses or make their living in the building renovation field. The interviews proved one thing right away: there is no "typical" building renovation in Chicago. Some people spend a few hundred dollars to decorate and maintain an old house, others spend tens of thousands. Some redesign the original interior, others meticulously restore it. Some people complete most of the repair work themselves, and others rely entirely on professional labor. The greatest variation lies in the problems people encounter. One house owner in the heart of Chicago watched his new patio collapse into a century-old covered outhouse pit. Another discovered a Prohibition-era still behind a wall.

Each renovation is a unique experience, and yet certain problems are almost inevitable. Renovators commented again and again: "It took longer than we thought it would." "It cost more than we had estimated." "Contractors never did the work when they had promised it." "At one point I wished I had never bought the house." Every renovator emphasized the frustrations of bringing a blighted building back to life. It requires great forebearance to live in mess and uncertainty for months or even years. A few harassed couples actually stopped their renovations because their marriages were taking such a beating from the strain.

Everyone mentioned the hardships of renovating, especially those who lived in the house while work was going on. Yet many seemed to relish their painful memories. They described — and laughed about — life under the most adverse conditions: snow falling into bedrooms through holes in the roof, no working plumbing but a tub and toilet, sultry summers and glacial winters. They recounted their horror stories with great pride, and seemed to appreciate their house all the more for their efforts.

Some among this group contracted the malady known as "rehabber's habit" or "old house fever." They became obsessed with their renovation, forsaking vacations and weekend trips and spending every spare dollar on their old house. Sometimes they talked as if the building was a venerable — and venerated — member of the family. In many cases these people went on to buy and renovate other dilapidated buildings, and some even became professional contractors.

Even the most committed renovators had some complaints, however, generally regarding the irresponsibility of contractors and laborers. It was a rare homeowner who did not report at least one bad experience with a professional. Contractors scrimped on their work, damaged property or finished work months behind schedule. Professionals with sterling reputations botched jobs for no apparent reason. Building owners learned that no professional was *guaranteed* to do a competent job. The suppliers and contractors named in this book were recommended by experienced renovators, but even they cannot be relied upon always to do high-quality work.

A second problem surfaced as the interviews continued: sometimes expert opinions were in conflict. On the issue of converting an old gas fireplace into a woodburning fireplace, for example, some experts recommended conversion, and others warned against it. Neither opinion was right, and neither was wrong. Since every old house is unique, a technique that works for one individual may fail for another. This is why *Old House Handbook* urges so strongly that renovators seek as much information from different sources as they can before jumping into anything risky or expensive. When opinions differ as to a repair and you have to make a decision, you need as much understanding of the matter as you can get.

Not much in a renovation is cut-and-dried. One repair forms the basis on which the next repair can be made; one design or decorating decision influences the next one and the one after that. Because renovations contain so many overlaps, *Old House Handbook* may touch on the subject you are most interested in several times, in different chapters. Information bearing on plumbing repair, for example, can be found both in Chapter Three and in Chapter Eight. Information on roofing is given in Chapters Three, Seven and Nine. *Old House Handbook* includes a detailed table of contents to help you find the information you need, but let your common sense guide you, too. If a chapter heading sounds like it might contain information useful to you, read the chapter!

One final note: to Chicago renovators, "old" can mean a variety of things. It can refer to a light and airy Queen Anne, a massive masonry gothic, a balloon-frame cottage or a dignified stucco or brownstone. It can refer to a house built as early as 1860 or to one built as late as

1940. It can mean a building that needs a paint job and a new kitchen floor or one that needs a complete overhaul inside and out. If you are looking for an "old" house or have recently purchased one, chances are, given Chicago history, that it dates from the 1880s or '90s. Because so many Chicago buildings were constructed in those decades, *Old House Handbook* often substitutes "Victorian" for "old" (Victoria ruled England from 1837 to 1901). Another large group of "old" Chicago buildings dates from the turn of the century to 1928. Building was light throughout the Depression, and after 1940 mechanical improvements in heating and cooling (among other things) brought an end to the high-ceilinged spaciousness that we associate with an "older" home. So your old house may not, strictly speaking, be "Victorian"; by East Coast standards it may not be "old" at all. But if your house was built before World War II and if it needs some work, *Old House Handbook* was written for you.

Although many individual craftsmen and old house owners were interviewed to prepare this book, a number of people deserve special thanks for their help and generosity:

PHIL COLLINS	Vice-President Uptown Federal Savings
LEONARD CURRIS	Dean Emeritus School of Architecture UICC
MAURICE FORKET	President Old Town Triangle Association
LONN FRYE	Architect, President Old Wicker Park Com.
CHUCK KING	King Chimney & Fireplace Co.
WILLIAM LAVICKA	Structural Engineer, Historic Boulevard Services
FRED LINDSTROM	Director of Rehabilitation Services, Department of Planning, City and Community Development, City of Chicago
DAN MADORI	General Contractor
STEVE PEYTON	Peyton LTD., Chairman Benjamin F. Ferguson Association
DON ZYGAS	Space Interiors

The Old House Handbook for Chicago and Suburbs

1

How a Neighborhood Revives

Most people find it difficult to believe the affluent and fashionable neighborhood in the western shadows of the John Hancock and Water Tower Place buildings was once a woe-begone, low-income neighborhood. In fact, it was. By the eve of World War I this stately old neighborhood had become rundown and tacky, not a slum but a bohemia. Today this area (known officially as the Near North Side) partakes of the glamorous and opulent ambience surrounding the "Magnificent Mile" of North Michigan Avenue. Similarly, visitors to the tree-lined streets of elegant old houses in Old Town, Mid-North and Lincoln Park West cannot imagine a time when these communities were anything but affluent and exclusive. Yet there was a time, in the not so distant past, when the director of a community organization in Lincoln Park confessed: "This is a community that could go either way." Lincoln Park, like the Near North Side, has come full circle — from affluence to poverty and back to affluence.

People tend to look at a neighborhood without a sense of time or history. They assume a neighborhood has pretty much always been as it now appears. But neighborhoods are not static. On the contrary, they are constantly changing, either for better or worse.

The process of neighborhood change, whether deterioration or re-covery, usually occurs in a sequence with different kinds of residents in each stage. Urban scholars refer to this process of change as "ur-ban ecological progression" because, as in natural ecologies, each group of residents creates the conditions for its replacement by the successive group. Understanding how a neighborhood changes is an invaluable tool for anyone trying to assess the future of an older neighborhood, and the revival of Chicago's North Side is an excel-lent example of neighborhood change by stages.

Chicago's North Side revival began in the area between Michigan and LaSalle and between the Chicago River and Division, an area originally settled as an upper-income community. This was the neigh-borhood of William Ogden, builder of railroads and Chicago's first mayor; Walter Newberry, whose fortune built the Newberry Li-brary; Samuel Nickelson, banker and art collector; and so many McCormicks that the neighborhood was called "McCormickville." But McCormickville lost its luster in the eyes of Chicago's affluent after the development of the Gold Coast, northeast of the Near North, during the last two decades of the nineteenth century. As the wealthy moved from McCormickville and were replaced by residents of lesser means, property owners cut back on building maintenance, businesses with dwindling clienteles abandoned the area, landlords subdivided the big mansions while once posh hotels became board-ing houses for transients. As the gaslight era gave way to electricity and automobiles, the once-fashionable Near North Side had become a neighborhood of the poor.

Still, even in poverty McCormickville was not a community with-out attractions. Housing, while in need of repair, was cheap and commodious, meals at local Italian restaurants were cheap and am-ple, and the area was conveniently near the Loop. With the virtues of cheap housing and services, McCormickville, by the eve of World War I, had become a haven for Chicago's artists and writers, and it had become known by a new name: Towertown, after the gothic watertower that stands in the middle of the Near North Side.

Many of Chicago's greatest cultural luminaries lived in Towertown at one time or another. Sherwood Anderson wrote his *Winesburg, Ohio* while living in a Wabash Street boardinghouse that he called "the little brother of the arts." Ben Hecht was one of Towertown's better known celebrities. Even Ernest Hemingway lived briefly in Towertown after World War I. Julio DeDiego, a Spanish painter who became popular in the Thirties, had a studio in the Italian Court Building on North Michigan Avenue. The Italian Court was itself something of a cultural mecca. Besides housing many Chicago writers and artists, the Italian Court contained the Gourmet Restaurant, a poets' rendezvous. At the Gourmet one could often find Vachel Lindsay, Edgar Lee Masters, Robert Frost, Alfred Kreymborg, Harriet Monroe or Carl Sandburg.

Towertown was attractive to residents not solely because of its low cost of living but for its freedom from the conventions of bourgeois America as well. The community became a refuge for social revolutionaries — labor radicals and organizers, socialists, pacifists, advocates of free love, atheists and anti-materialists. As a bohemia, the area became an attraction in itself. Curiosity and adventure seekers from all over the city came to Towertown to observe and indulge in the unconventional culture of the community. At popular Towertown bistros, like the Dill Pickle on Tooker's Alley near La-Salle, people would come to see an original play by Ben Hecht, to hear poetry, to listen to radical politics, or to celebrity-watch. Later in the Twenties, Rush Street mansions were renovated and converted to speakeasies for the forbidden pleasures of Towertown visitors.

Following the Depression and World War II, the redevelopment of Towertown resumed and was all but assured after the "Magnificent Mile" redevelopment project was announced for Michigan Avenue. The mansions of McCormickville and the boarding houses of Towertown became some of Chicago's most popular and expensive restaurants, boutiques and galleries. By the middle of the Fifties, the

Near North Side was fashionable again, although the commercial intrusion of Michigan Avenue prevented the area from becoming a true residential community. By the end of the decade, few Chicagoans even remembered the name Towertown, much less the bohemian Towertown community. For the artists, writers and bohemians who had initiated redevelopment a half century before, the Near North had become too expensive for their budgets and too commercial for their tastes; they moved on.

While the Near North Side was undergoing a revival during the post-World War II years, the community farther north, known as Old Town, was rapidly decaying. The 1950 census revealed that over twenty-seven percent of the buildings in the Lincoln Park area, of which Old Town is a part, were substandard — without running water or toilets or structurally unsound. However, Old Town's low cost of living and spacious though dilapidated housing was an attraction to the writers and artists who could no longer afford the Near North Side. Thus during the late 1940s a new artists' colony began forming in Old Town.

As on the Near North Side twenty years earlier, the unconventional atmosphere of Old Town soon attracted new investors. Individuals of middle income, many of them teachers, college professors, media professionals, or young architects, were among the first to buy buildings in Old Town for renovation. Their professions and incomes are typical of a group often referred to as "urban pioneers." Urban pioneers want a stimulating cultural environment and are not intimidated by deterioration or blight. In Old Town, they saw worth in the stately old buildings, and they were willing to gamble on the neighborhood's future.

In 1949 the new renovators and some long-time property owners formed an organization to aid their community's revival — the Old Town Triangle Association. The Association's annual art and craft street fair soon became an established tradition in Chicago and successfully attracted new residents to the community. By the mid-

Fifties, the revived Old Town had acquired an old title that had belonged to Towertown before — the Greenwich Village of Chicago.

Several years after redevelopment started in Old Town, renovation spread north as urban pioneers began to discover the community immediately adjacent to Old Town: Mid-North. As in Old Town before it, the residents of Mid-North attracted more renovators and restored the faith of old residents in the neighborhood's future by forming a community organization, the Mid-North Association, and by sponsoring neighborhood events. Yet, while renovation increased throughout Old Town and Mid-North, deterioration continued unabated in other parts of Lincoln Park. To reverse the spread of blight, the Old Town Triangle Association and the Mid-North Association formed, in 1954, the Lincoln Park Conservation Association and sought federal assistance for urban renewal. Two years later Lincoln Park was declared a Conservation Area and plans were made for urban renewal projects throughout the community. Lincoln Park's prospects improved immediately. Major Lincoln Park institutions — McCormick Theological Seminary, Francis Parker School, Aetna State Bank and DePaul University — all facing the decision to expand or to move to the suburbs, opted to stay in Lincoln Park and expand.

By the 1960s over 300 units had been renovated in Old Town and a similar number in the Mid-North area. In addition, the government had embarked on a major renewal program in the central section of Lincoln Park. Ogden Avenue north of North Avenue was converted into a mall for commercial, residential and institutional use. Land between Dickens and Webster was cleared for a park. New houses were built along Larrabee Street, and government-subsidized home improvement loans were made available to all building owners in the urban renewal area. As the Sixties progressed, the pace of renovation in Lincoln Park accelerated faster than anyone had believed possible.

After a decade of redevelopment in Old Town and Mid-North,

property values, taxes and rents began to escalate, causing the community to become too expensive for less affluent artists and writers. The art colony that had given Old Town its character and reputation was forced to migrate to cheaper neighborhoods north and west. Lincoln Avenue near DePaul University became the center of a new art colony and youth counter-culture that was remarkably similar to the Towertown bohemia of half a century before. And, like Towertown and Old Town, the atmosphere of Lincoln Avenue attracted new, more affluent residents to the surrounding neighborhood. During the late Sixties, teachers, professionals in advertising and public relations, professors and architects began renovating the old row houses and brick two-flats throughout the DePaul neighborhood. By the early Seventies much of the DePaul area had been completely renovated and building values were inflating rapidly. As the neighborhood grew in popularity, the original urban pioneers were bought out by more affluent bankers, lawyers and upper-echelon business executives. In the course of a single decade, the DePaul neighborhood had experienced nearly complete redevelopment.

The DePaul neighborhood was not alone in its renaissance. The community immediately north of Lincoln Park, Lake View, was also benefiting from Lincoln Park's redevelopment. Small businesses appealing to the young and affluent opened along Broadway, while young families renovated buildings throughout the previously depressed south central Lake View area. The march of redevelopment continued north.

There has been continuity and direction to the redevelopment of Chicago's North Side. Redevelopment has occurred in distinct and discernible stages. The first stage of neighborhood rebirth usually starts with artists, writers and others who desire an alternative lifestyle. The artists are usually followed by the first building renovators, the urban pioneers. As the urban pioneers make a blighted neighborhood pleasant again, the area becomes attractive to more affluent people. Real-estate interests rather than home owners begin to renovate buildings on a larger scale. Bankers, lawyers and business executives replace the artists and pioneer renovators who initiated the neighborhood revival. Redevelopment spreads just as deterioration does, block by block, community by community. When one block is discovered by building renovators, interest in adjoining blocks soon follows. As development progresses and the cost-of-living in a community escalates, middle-income residents are forced to move to less expensive neighboring communities, stimulating economic uplift there as well.

The phenomenon of neighborhood regeneration that occurred on Chicago's North Side is not unique to Chicago. It has occurred in a similar fashion in other American cities—Georgetown in Washington, D.C., Society Hill in Philadelphia and Greenwich Village in New York. People who understand how a neighborhood revives and who can recognize the first signs of regeneration are likely to profit from their knowledge and foresight. The optimum time to buy into a reviving neighborhood is in the earliest stages, when buildings are inexpensive and the area still appears blighted and forlorn. When a neighborhood becomes generally known as "hot," buildings become increasingly less a bargain. A neighborhood regeneration ends with the Johnnie-come-latelys buying the least attractive buildings at the highest prices.

REDEVELOPING NEIGHBORHOODS

1 Gold Coast
2 Near North
3 Old Town
4 Mid North
5 Lincoln Park West
6 Lincoln Central
7 Wrightwood
8 DePaul - Sheffield
9 RANCH
10 East Lake View
11 South Central Lake View
12 North Lake View
13 Uptown
14 East Ravenswood
15 Edgewater
16 Andersonville
17 Rodgers Park
18 Ravenswood
19 Wicker Park
20 North Wicker Park
21 East Humboldt Park
22 Logan Square
23 Near West
24 Pilsen
25 Kenwood
26 Hyde Park
27 Jackson Park Highlands
28 East South Shore
29 Pullman
30 Morgan Park
31 Beverly

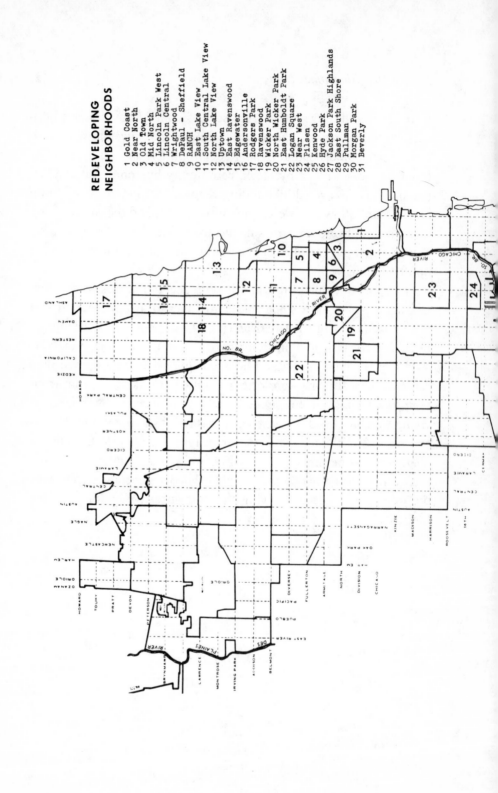

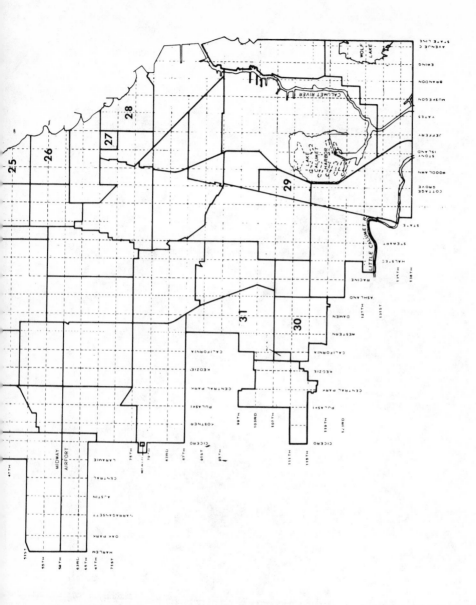

The "Chicago Cottage" is found in the oldest Chicago neighborhoods such as Old Town, the Near West Side and Pilsen. It is distinguished by wood-frame construction atop a high masonry basement, with a high front entrance.

2

Old Neighborhoods to Consider

Buying a house in an older, still-blighted city neighborhood is not the same as buying a house elsewhere. People purchasing a house in a suburb or stable city neighborhood base their decision on the community as it appears; people buying in an old and deteriorated city neighborhood base their decision on what they hope the neighborhood will become. Anyone buying a house in an older depressed neighborhood must possess a willingness to await the community's redevelopment and to accept the risk that the community may not redevelop at all. The following Chicago neighborhoods are now in some stage of redevelopment or, according to some expert opinion, are soon likely to be.

(Important note: Although the words *community* and *neighborhood* are commonly used interchangeably, in this chapter there is an important distinction. A *community* is an area officially designated by the City for government purposes [for example, for census taking]. The seventy-six official communities of Chicago have designated names and boundaries. A *neighborhood* is simply the area residents think of as their small part of the city. A neighborhood is therefore smaller and more ambiguous than a community and often has more than one name. For example, Sheffield and DePaul are al-

ternative names for the same neighborhood in the Lincoln Park
community, and Wicker Park and East Humboldt Park are overlapping neighborhoods in the West Town community. Thus *community* is a more precise term than *neighborhood*).

LINCOLN PARK

The official boundaries of Lincoln Park are North Avenue on the
south, the north branch of the Chicago River to the west, Diversey
on the north, and the park, Lincoln Park, to the east. Within the
larger community are seven generally recognized smaller neighborhoods — Old Town in the southeast, Mid-North in the east central, Lincoln Park West in the northeast, Wrightwood in the northwest, Sheffield in the west central, RANCH in the southwest, and
Lincoln Center between Old Town and RANCH.

In Old Town and Mid-North, building renovation for the most
part ended some years ago when few buildings were left unrenovated. Lincoln Park West, where little deterioration occurred anyway, has few unrenovated buildings remaining either. Only the fortunate few for whom income is not a limitation can consider purchasing a building in these neighborhoods.

The Sheffield or DePaul neighborhood is following a similar path.
There are few unrenovated buildings left in Sheffield and, with soar-
ing land values, even these are becoming expensive. There is in this
some irony. A century ago the working-class people who lived in
Sheffield looked east and dreamed of living on the Gold Coast or
in Mid-North with the wealthy few. A century later it is only the
wealthy who can afford to buy in Sheffield.

The only Lincoln Park neighborhoods where buildings remain
available at reasonable prices are Wrightwood, Lincoln Center and
RANCH.

Wrightwood is bounded by Halsted on the east, Diversey on the
north, Fullerton on the south and Lakewood on the west. Since it is

contiguous with two recently redeveloped neighborhoods, Sheffield and Lincoln Park West, Wrightwood has become increasingly attractive to renovators of more moderate means. Buildings in Wrightwood include the mix typical of Lincoln Park — brick row houses, masonry buildings with granite, limestone, sandstone or brick facades, and wood-frame houses; there are fewer large apartment buildings here than in other Lincoln Park neighborhoods. Southern Wrightwood has the best masonry buildings, along Lill, Wrightwood and Altgeld, while wood-frame houses predominate in north Wrightwood.

While Wrightwood escaped the deterioration that plagued other Lincoln Park neighborhoods, the area has suffered from many ill-advised building "modernizations." On entire blocks in Wrightwood almost every building has been covered with asphalt panels, fiber-board, perma-stone or aluminum siding. The original and attractive appearance of these buildings has been demeaned by phony exterior coverings. People buying such houses in Wrightwood will have to plan on substantial exterior restoration if they want an attractive old house that looks like an old house. Several recent renovators in Wrightwood have done such restorations, and if the trend continues, the neighborhood's original charm will return.

Lincoln Center, immediately west of Old Town and Mid-North, experienced more urban renewal demolition and reconstruction than any other neighborhood in Lincoln Park. Those parts of Lincoln Center that were not demolished are now nearly fully renovated. However, a few "modernized" wood-frame buildings still remain. Though an expenditure to restore the exterior will be necessary, these buildings may still prove to be a good buy.

RANCH, named for the neighborhood's street boundaries —Racine, North Avenue, Clybourn and Halsted — has been the last Lincoln Park neighborhood to undergo extensive renovation. Most recent renovation has been in northern RANCH, along Dayton, Fremont and Bissell. Unfortunately RANCH experienced extensive

The "Chicago Graystone" is rather austere when compared to other Victorian styles. Yet Graystones usually have high ceilings, natural woodwork and fireplaces. The streets of Lake View, Uptown, Logan Square and East Humboldt Park are lined with Graystones.

deterioration and demolition before Lincoln Park began to redevelop, and much of the area near North Avenue and along Clybourn is now vacant. Still, a few buildings suitable for renovation exist north of Willow on Sheffield, Dayton, Fremont and Bissell.

Lincoln Park is Chicago's number-one community success story. It is now "the" place to live in Chicago. Prospective buyers need not worry about an investment in Lincoln Park. However, few people interested in buying an old city house can afford Lincoln Park anymore. And with many people still interested in buying an old house in the city, the question arises: what neighborhood will they turn to?

LAKE VIEW

As Lincoln Park has become increasingly expensive and exclusive, more renovators have purchased buildings in Lake View. Lake View has a wide variety of neighborhoods, from the affluent lakefront on the east to the working-class bungalow belt in the west. Bounded by Diversey on the south, the Chicago and Northwestern Railroad on the west, Irving Park Road and Montrose on the north and Lake Michigan on the east, Lake View has never been a real slum; in fact, overdevelopment has always been the main problem in the eastern part of the community. However, in the mid-Sixties portents of blight became evident in south central and especially in northern Lake View bordering Uptown. Before deterioration progressed very far, however, escalating rents in Lincoln Park caused an influx of middle-income residents into southeast Lake View. As more people of greater means moved into the community, real-estate developers assembled and rehabilitated whole blocks of multi-unit apartment buildings. By the mid-Seventies redevelopment had spread between Clark and Broadway as far north as Addison Avenue.

The best areas of Lake View for renovation are east central, south central, central and north central. East and south east Lake View have already become very expensive.

East central and north central Lake View, roughly the area between Halsted and Clark and between Belmont and Irving Park
Road, has a good mix of two-story frame and masonry buildings.
Along Newport west of Halsted are many excellent three-flat masonry buildings still at reasonable prices. There is also a selection of
one- and two-unit buildings along Wilton, Fremont and Reta in
the neighborhood around Wrigley Field. As one moves north, deterioration becomes increasingly evident. Nevertheless, most obser-
vers expect renovation to continue and eventually to reach the northern limits of the community.

South central Lake View, the area around Racine south of Belmont, has become increasingly popular with people who cannot afford neighboring Lincoln Park. South central Lake View is an area
of predominantly wood-frame construction. (When the neighborhood was developed, it was a northern suburb that allowed the wood-
frame construction prohibited in post-fire Chicago.) The potential
of these Victorian wood-frame houses is often lost on casual observ-
ers since most of them have been defaced with false sidings. Fortunately, several recent building renovations in the area have included
attractive exterior restorations that may inspire similar restorations
by new residents.

In addition to the already mentioned Lake View neighborhoods,
there are several others that may be of interest to people desiring an
old house in need of little repair or renovation. The best of these
neighborhoods are Central Lake View and Northwest Lake View.

Central Lake View east of Ashland Avenue has many stately old
buildings, as travelers to and from Wrigley Field on Addison Avenue can attest. From Ashland to Racine and along such sidestreets
as Greenview and Bosworth, Central Lake View is a mix of large
Victorian houses in different architectural styles and in both masonry
and wood construction. Northwest Lake View, the area north of
Irving Park Road, east of Ashland Avenue and west of Graceland
Cemetery, has many Victorian and turn-of-the-century buildings

equal to the best buildings of Lincoln Park in all respects but one —
the Lake View buildings are much less expensive. Central and
Northwest Lake View are much more than a long walk from the
lakefront and are undeservedly obscure, but at the rate East and
south central Lake View are redeveloping, it is not unlikely that the
central and northwestern parts of the neighborhood will be "discovered" by people desiring an old house in Chicago's North Side.

UPTOWN

A new city college was built recently in Uptown, complete with
lawns and young shade trees. The trees died. But more than just
trees die in Uptown. By any measure Uptown is not the worst community in Chicago, but it has gained the most notorious reputation.
Within the recent past Uptown has been the setting for a novel,
City Dogs, by Chicagoan Bill Brashler and a successful Broadway
play, "American Buffalo" by Chicagoan David Mamet, that high-
lighted the sordid mix of poverty and desperation that characterize
Uptown.

Despite Uptown's infamy, it has adherents who believe the community will redevelop in the same fashion as Lincoln Park. Uptown
is adjacent to Lake Michigan and Chicago's most appealing park,
Lincoln Park. Transportation from Uptown to the Loop is excellent.
And though most buildings are dilapidated, they possess the amenities so sought-after by old house renovators — fireplaces, large rooms,
high ceilings and natural woodwork. In fact, Uptown was originally a genteel upper-class community, as its baroque movie palaces
and ballrooms suggest.

Besides its innate attractions, Uptown — as its boosters point
out — is the last chance renovators of moderate means have on Chicago's North Side. Figuratively, Uptown is the last frontier for the
urban pioneer. The communities north of Uptown are stable while
those to the south are redeveloping and hence experiencing a boom

Two houses in Italianate style — a wood structure on the North Side
and a masonry house on the Near West Side. Italianate architecture
can be recognized by extended eaves with ornate brackets
and rounded windows and porches.

in building values. Uptown's supporters argue, therefore, that Uptown almost certainly will redevelop.

However, there are crucial differences between Uptown and the redeveloping North Side communities. Lincoln Park revived through the combined efforts of a great many single-home renovators. It was only when regeneration was virtually assured that real estate interests began rehabilitating the larger multi-unit apartment buildings. Uptown, unlike Lincoln Park, is predominantly a community of large multi-unit buildings. These buildings are too expensive for the middle-income owner to renovate, and real-estate developers do not spend money on rehabilitation unless they are certain of attracting affluent tenants.

The most likely course for Uptown is for redevelopment to start in the southeast as neighboring Lake View becomes more expensive. As more affluent people move into southeast Uptown, developers will rehabilitate apartment buildings, new development will fill the many vacant lots, and the commercial center along Broadway and Wilson will redevelop to appeal to the new, wealthier populace. However, this movement northward may be slow, and it probably will not extend to northwest Uptown until the revival of the southeast is realized.

For the prospective renovator willing to brave Uptown, finding a suitable building in southeast Uptown may be difficult. There are few single-family homes there, and those that are available may seem unreasonably expensive. Zoning is to blame for this; the area east of Broadway is zoned for high-density development (skyscrapers) so the land is considerably more valuable than the buildings that stand upon it. For people of moderate incomes who are interested in southeast Uptown, probably the best course is to join with someone else in purchasing a 2-, 3-, or 4-flat and then to rent or sell the extra units. There are many old multi-unit buildings, most of them built during the first two decades of the twentieth century, along Kenmore, Belle Plaine, Buena, and Gordon Terrace.

Single-family dwellings are more numerous and less expensive in west-central Uptown, between Lawrence and Montrose and between Broadway and the Chicago and Northwestern Railroad. The area west of Clark, the East Ravenswood Conservation Area, has an excellent mix of big stately wood-frame and masonry buildings. Although deterioration has been controlled in East Ravenswood, it is a long way from the Lake and from Lincoln Park, and therefore may be a long time in redeveloping.

Though the official northern boundary of Uptown is Devon Avenue, the area north of Foster and east of Clark in Uptown is more commonly known as Edgewater, and the area north of Foster and west of Clark is usually referred to as Andersonville. Edgewater and Andersonville are stable neighborhoods with many fine old buildings. However, the prospective buyer in these neighborhoods should be aware that large renovation costs might not be recoverable when the building is sold. Building values throughout the neighborhood may not increase to cover the original renovation costs.

In short, Uptown has many grand old buildings, but it is not a neighborhood for the timorous.

WICKER PARK

Wicker Park is an obscure inner city neighborhood whose only recognition has derived from its most famous resident — Frank Majcinek, better known as "Frankie Machine," small time hustler and drug addict, the man with the golden arm. Nelson Algren, the literary procreator of Frank Majcinek and a longtime denizen of Wicker Park himself, assesses the neighborhood in *The Man With the Golden Arm* as static and unchanging: "Neither God, war, nor the ward super work any deep change on West Division Street." That may have been true in 1951 but not in recent years. On the contrary, during the last decade the character of Wicker Park has changed rapidly, beginning with an ethnic change in the 1960s from

Wicker Park has large mansion-like houses on lots larger than those of similar buildings on the lakefront.

East European to Puerto Rican. Blight soon followed. Now after a decade of deterioration and demolition, there are signs that a revival is underway.

Wicker Park (with boundaries of Western Avenue on the west, Division on the south, Milwaukee Avenue on the east and the Chicago, Milwaukee, St. Paul and Pacific Railroad on the north) is something of a Chicago oddity. It was built as a wealthy and exclusive community, and yet its history was never recorded. Many of the Wicker Park mansions, as expensive and opulent as any on the Gold Coast, were demolished without even a photograph to record their passing. Most Chicagoans if they think about this neighborhood at all, assume it is just part of Chicago's banal bungalow belt. It is not.

Wicker Park has a number of attractions that make revival likely. It is ten minutes from the Loop by public transportation. Most of its buildings are single-family or small apartment buildings of the masonry construction preferred by renovators. And most important, with Lincoln Park so fully renovated and expensive, it is one of the few city neighborhoods available to renovators of moderate means.

In fact, Wicker Park may already be in the first stages of regeneration. For some years young middle-income professionals with families have been buying and renovating buildings throughout Wicker Park. As in Old Town and Mid-North, the new residents of Wicker Park have created an organization to promote the neighborhood through publicity campaigns and by sponsoring community events. The extent of their success at neighborhood improvement is not yet easily seen since most renovation work thus far has been limited to interiors.

Despite the stirrings of revival in Wicker Park, skeptics, and they are legion, point out that with the exception of the urban renewal project around Circle Campus, no Chicago community has successfully redeveloped that was not adjacent to the Lake. There is no big park in Wicker Park, and deterioration is already far advanced, with unoccupied buildings and vacant lots on nearly every block. Certainly there is a risk in buying in Wicker Park.

For those willing to accept the risk, the streets with the best buildings are Hoyne, LeMoyne, Schiller, Evergreen, Leavitt and Potomac. More modest but still appealing brick buildings line Crystal, Bell and Oakley. The area of Wicker Park east of Damen has suffered more blight and demolition; however, there are still some fine old dwellings on Wicker Park Avenue and Wolcott.

If Wicker Park does repeat the sensational success of Lincoln Park, the people who risked buying while the neighborhood was blighted will have the most to gain — the best buildings, in the most desirable locations, at the best price. On the other hand, if Wicker Park continues to deteriorate, all its residents will have gained is the dubious distinction of having lived in the same neighborhood as Frank Majcinek.

EAST HUMBOLDT PARK AND NORTH WICKER PARK

There is considerable contention among Chicago's urban experts as to whether Wicker Park will redevelop. However there is no disagreement that if the Near Northwest Side does redevelop, it will start first in Wicker Park. Hence the future of two other West Town neighborhoods, East Humboldt Park and North Wicker Park, depends on the revival of Wicker Park, for redevelopment will spread to surrounding neighborhoods only if Wicker Park becomes increasingly expensive.

The area north of Milwaukee Avenue and south of the Chicago, Milwaukee, St. Paul and Pacific Railroad is an old Polish neighborhood nicknamed Bucktown, allegedly because so many Polish immigrants furtively kept goats (a buck is a male goat). The neighborhood has since been renamed North Wicker Park, probably by real-estate interests wanting a more glamorous name to promote the area. Most buildings in this neighborhood are not as desirable as those in neighboring Wicker Park. They have fewer elegant architectural features, occupy smaller lots, and are often below street grade. Still, they are as good as most buildings in Lincoln Park which are three times as expensive.

The neighborhood immediately west of Wicker Park, the western section of West Town, is known to its residents as East Humboldt Park, after the park that forms its western boundary. If redevelopment does not come soon to East Humboldt Park, little will remain to redevelop. In recent years this neighborhood has sustained massive demolition, usually as the consequence of arson, which is all very unfortunate as the buildings were mostly solid and appealing old dwellings. Redevelopment, should it come, will probably come first to the area nearest Wicker Park, though many of the neighborhood's finest buildings lie farther west, near Humboldt Part itself.

LOGAN SQUARE

During an era in Chicago's history when the city was really trying to live up to its motto, "a city in the park," a series of parks and connecting boulevards were developed on the city's outskirts. Along these spacious and sylvan boulevards the wealthy built their mansions. Since that elegant gas-light era, the city's periphery has moved many miles west and north, and so have the rich. But the mansions remain, and some of the best grace the boulevards of Logan Square.

Logan Square is the community immediately north of West Town, with boundaries of Diversey to the north, the Kennedy Expressway on the east and the Chicago, Milwaukee, St. Paul and Pacific Railroad on the south and west. Like Wicker Park and East Humboldt Park, Logan Square has been undergoing an ethnic transformation from East European to Puerto Rican within the last decade. So far, however, it has successfully resisted the blight that plagues other Near Northwest Side neighborhoods.

Recently, young professionals priced out of the Lincoln Park housing market have been purchasing some of the mansions along Kedzie Parkway, Humboldt Boulevard, Palmer Square, Kedzie

Logan Square has boulevards of large mansion-like houses that have generally been well-maintained.

Boulevard and Logan Boulevard, but whether the entire community will redevelop is not yet certain. The great liability of Logan Square is that its beauty is only skin deep. Within half a block of the boulevards, especially in the area between Fullerton and North Avenue, ornate mansions give way to commonplace bungalows that most potential renovators find unappealing. Away from the boulevards, the most appealing neighborhood of Logan Square lies between Fullerton and Diversey, particularly west of Kedzie Boulevard. Many fine nineteenth-century wood-frame and masonry buildings are available in this west Logan Square neighborhood.

NEAR WEST SIDE

In the early 1970s a few Near West Side residents suggested that they promote their neighborhood's redevelopment with a new and more descriptive name. As the community is still known by the vague and vapid name of Near West Side, evidently no one gave the suggestion much thought. They should have, for this community has not received the attention it deserves.

The revival of the Near West Side began in the early 1960s with the construction of the University of Illinois Circle Campus. The new West Side Medical Complex on the neighborhood's western borders and the university on the east displaced and embittered a great many original residents, but at the same time stimulated a badly depressed economy. Doctors, professors and staff professionals at both institutions became interested in the begrimed old houses near their work, and the city's Urban Renewal department encouraged renovation as well as new construction. Once redevelopment was under way, longtime Italian residents began to renovate and upgrade their property. Ten years after the Near West Side project began, the ill-famed neighborhood of Jane Addams and Sam Giancana had acquired a new reputation and a new appeal.

Though there are still many old and unrenovated buildings

This Near West Side building is an example of Mansard or Second
Empire architecture.

throughout the Near West Side, strangers often have a hard time buying them. The Near West Side has a very old and rooted Italian community that tries to sustain itself by selling buildings only to family, friends or other Italian residents. Most recent non-Italian residents have been accommodated with new housing on cleared urban renewal land. For those interested in an old building in the Near West Side, the best approach is to make the acquaintance of residents and community leaders. A building is more likely to be found by word-of-mouth than by any conventional means.

PILSEN

One of the great street scenes left in Chicago is found in Pilsen, along 18th Street between Ashland and Halsted. Especially at the intersection of Blue Island, 18th Street is a vibrant reminder of an earlier Chicago. If it were not for the ubiquitous automobile, one could easily imagine himself in nineteenth-century Chicago. One of the oldest neighborhoods in the city, Pilsen was built for the most part before the street grades were raised. There is a suggestion of the Old World or of New York in Pilsen, with its tall two- and three-story brick buildings, closely-spaced and near the street and with community life oriented towards the sidewalk.

Pilsen, with boundaries of Halsted on the east, Damen on the west, Cermak on the south and the Burlington Northern Railroad on the north, is a neighborhood in the Lower West Side. As its name suggests, Pilsen was originally settled by East Europeans, mostly Bohemians. In the early 1960s Mexicans began moving in, many of them displaced by urban renewal from the Near West Side. Now the neighborhood is known for its Mexican restaurants and for the Chicago artists who have moved their studios to Halsted Street. Few experts, however, believe that Pilsen will redevelop immediately. Unlike most neighborhoods that have redeveloped, Pilsen was built for the working-class. Pilsen has nineteenth-century charm, but it

Pilsen is an old neighborhood of closely-spaced masonry buildings,
most below street grade. Pilsen has some of the most
attractive cornices in Chicago.

does not have nineteenth-century opulence. In addition, most of its buildings are below street grade and close to the sidewalk; thus, few buildings are graced with lawns, and few streets have landscaped, tree-lined parkways. Whether such a neighborhood will ever gain favor with Chicago's middle-class is a matter of some doubt.

Most experts believe Uptown and Wicker Park are more likely to redevelop than Pilsen in the near future. Pilsen's prospects are probably tied to the success of the proposed South Loop New Town. Residents of the South Loop community might find Pilsen attractive as an entertainment and commercial district, triggering regeneration throughout Pilsen. But this scenario lies several decades away.

HYDE PARK-KENWOOD

Urban renewal projects have generally been marked with controversy and often acrimony, but none so much as the urban renewal of Hyde Park-Kenwood. By the mid-1950s, Hyde Park and Kenwood, the communities between 47th and the Midway Plaisance and between Cottage Grove Boulevard and the Lake, had almost succumbed to the blight that was consuming most of the South Side. When conventional efforts to arrest the blight failed, community organizations led by the University of Chicago sought government assistance in the form of urban renewal. In 1955 the Hyde Park-Kenwood urban renewal project began in force.

As the first and one of the largest urban renewal projects in the nation, Hyde Park-Kenwood became an urban laboratory. Several books were written about the project's methods, goals and results. One nationally recognized urbanologist used it as a paradigm of everything that can go wrong with urban renewal. Nevertheless, when the project was completed Hyde Park and Kenwood had been restored to something approaching their former elegance. Today these communities are regarded as the most cosmopolitan and intellectual in Chicago.

The Romanesque style followed and was a reaction to Queen Anne architecture. It was as simple as Queen Anne architecture was ornate. Romanesque architecture is marked by heavy massing, little ornamentation and especially arched windows or porches. There are thousands of Romanesques along the boulevards of the South Side.

Unfortunately the dynamics of redevelopment do not exist in Hyde Park or Kenwood. No one is predicting that these communities will revert to their pre-renewal blight; on the other hand, no one is predicting that redevelopment will soon spread to neighboring Woodlawn, Oakland or Grand Boulevard. Most people feel that Hyde Park-Kenwood is just holding its own. It is somewhat ironic that people are willing to invest such large sums in North Side buildings that have so little appeal compared to the typical building in Woodlawn, Oakland or Grand Boulevard. But people buy for the community as well as for the building, and the South Side suffers from the reputation of being a high crime area.

The person looking for an old building to renovate in Hyde Park-Kenwood faces a problem. In the original renewal area between the Midway and 47th Street most buildings have already been renovated, and nearby communities are very risky. Probably least risky is north Woodlawn, where the University of Chicago may finally commence its long-proposed south expansion. In this area, south of 63rd, there are several streets of attractive limestone-faced row houses. The remaining neighborhoods around Hyde Park and Kenwood, while they contain the most opulent mansions in Chicago, are still extremely risky for the lone renovator to chance.

PULLMAN

On the Far South Side of Chicago, just east of the Calumet Expressway at 111th Street, lies Pullman, a picturesque little community steeped in American history. Pullman was built in the 1880s as an industrial utopia by George Pullman, the Chicago multi-millionaire inventor and manufacturer of the railroad sleeping car. George Pullman hoped to end class strife and the need for labor unions by providing his workers with a pleasant place to live. With the design and direction of New York architect Solon S. Beman, Pullman built his company town with parks, library, theater, shopping center, school and church. Initially George Pullman's company town seemed a successful experiment in capitalistic paternalism, but his utopian dreams collapsed in the bitter labor strike of 1894 that still bears his name.

As the years passed Chicago expanded and engulfed Pullman, and by 1964 the community was deteriorating rapidly. In a response typical of government in this period, the City of Chicago recommended that Pullman be razed and cleared for industrial development. As in Old Town and other neighborhoods that have been threatened with urban renewal destruction, the government action spurred Pullman's residents into saving their community. Within a decade Pullman had won national and city landmark status and nearly twenty-five percent of the houses had been restored.

However, redevelopment in Pullman has remained pretty much a family affair. Although the community is attracting new residents, the impetus for its redevelopment has stemmed from first, second and third generation Pullmanites, many of whom have returned from the suburbs to the community of their roots. Most people interested in renovating an old city house will find Pullman inconvenient to the Loop and to the North Side Culture scene. However, for those who work on the Far South Side and would like to live there as well, the quaint little Queen Anne row houses are worth considering.

*   *   *

These neighborhoods are by no means the only ones in Chicago to boast fine old buildings in a pleasant atmosphere. But they are the neighborhoods where real estate values are appreciating, or soon will be, rapidly enough to justify considerable outlays for renovation and repair. Nevertheless, one should not rule out buying an old house in more stable neighborhoods simply because they lack a real estate boom. The charm and appeal of these neighborhoods is reason enough to live there, and further, most of their buildings are far superior to anything that can be found in the mass-constructed, single-design suburban subdivision.

On the Southwest Side, Beverly and Morgan Park have a nine-teenth-century suburban flavor with large, distinctive houses. Beverly is an uncommon area of Chicago with its rolling wooded hills and large old houses, many of landmark quality. Neighboring Morgan Park is an area of curved tree-lined streets with wonderful wood-frame Victorian houses, some in the style of San Francisco "gingerbread." Beverly and Morgan Park have not yet experienced any wide-spread deterioration although building values slumped in the early 1970s as confidence in the area waned with the approach of racial change. Complete confidence in Beverly or Morgan Park has not yet recovered, nor have building values, but the longer these communities avoid blight, the greater are their chances for revival.

On the North Side west of Lake View and Uptown are several old but stable neighborhoods, such as Ravenswood and Lincoln Square, comprised generally of more modest dwellings. Yet dispersed throughout these neighborhoods are many imposing old buildings, many built as country estates when Chicago's northern boundary was North Avenue. These obscure, old neighborhoods may never carry the most prestigious addresses in Chicago, but that does not diminish the charm or comfort of individual buildings in the neighborhoods.

On the Far North Side, Rogers Park is a multi-ethnic community with a lakefront proximity. Though free of any serious blight, Rogers Park has recently, as real estate people say, developed a soft mar-

This Rogers Park Queen Anne is typical of hundreds in the Chicago area, especially in Oak Park, Evanston, Rogers Park, Morgan Park, Beverly and Logan Square. Queen Anne was the most flamboyant Victorian architectural style, characterized by a heavy use of ornaments and a variety of shapes, sizes and planes in non-symmetrical patterns. Note that this house has six different window sizes in just one plane.

ket-building values have not kept up with increases in the general metropolitan housing market. The concern of community organizations and government is evident by the recent inclusion of East Rogers Park in several programs limited to blighted areas. The sagging real estate market of Rogers Park does offer the opportunity, with risk of course, of purchasing a reasonably-priced old house that could appreciate rapidly if the community revives. The area between Clark and Ridge is a pleasant neighborhood of large wood-frame houses with spacious lawns and in good repair.

SUBURBAN OPPORTUNITIES

Many older neighborhoods in Chicago are undeniably attractive and elegant, but splendid Victorian houses and pleasant old neighborhoods can be found in the suburbs as well. Many Chicago suburbs are as old as the city, and in fact, most old suburban housing was designed and built by the same architects and builders who built nineteenth-century Chicago. Therefore, renovating an old house in the suburbs is often very similar to renovating one in the city.

There are, however, a few differences. The building codes of most suburbs allow for owner repair and installation of plumbing and electrical service lines with usually only a follow-up building inspection, while Chicago does not. Suburbs are also usually more strict, even stringent, in building code enforcement. Building owners who leave even small amounts of construction or demolition debris in their garbage are often visited by the local Building Inspector looking for a permit shortly after the garbage is collected by the city. Nor are most suburbs as willing to brook building violations as the city. In some suburbs, if an owner does not correct his building violations, the local building department will make the necessary corrections and charge the owner for them. However, vigorous building code enforcement in the suburbs does not mean that suburban building departments are free of the same corruption that plagues city building owners. On the contrary, suburban building owners often encounter building inspectors who hint for a "gratuity" while searching for code violations.

People interested in renovating an old house in the suburbs should be sure that the cost of purchase and renovation does not exceed the average selling price of buildings in the suburb. Building values in the older suburbs are more stable and less subject to rapid increases than are redeveloping city neighborhoods. If one spends more to buy and renovate a building than the average selling price of other buildings in the suburb, he may not fully recover his money when the building is sold. To put it another way, a Lake Forest mansion in Cicero would sell at Cicero prices, not Lake Forest prices.

In some suburbs, another hazard in renovating an old house is the possibility of a staggering increase in property taxes. After a dilapidated building of little value is rehabilitated, it will soon be reassessed at a much higher value, causing property taxes to increase. While this is true in the city as well, most wealthier suburbs have significantly higher tax rates. Hence a person of modest means renovating a dilapidated house in a wealthy suburb may soon discover he cannot afford the taxes.

The best way to look for old houses in the suburbs is to follow the rails. During the Victorian era, railroads were the life lines of the suburbs. In fact where a railroad built a station, a suburb would germinate. Since few houses built in the nineteenth century were more than a reasonable walking distance from a train station, the way to search for old suburban houses is to follow the commuter railroads from the central city.

The Burlington Northern Railroad travels through several nineteenth-century suburbs southwest of Chicago, including Riverside, LaGrange, Hinsdale, Downers Grove and Naperville. The Chicago and Northwestern Railroad, western branch, travels through another set of Victorian villages including Elmhurst, Glen Ellyn, Lombard and Wheaton. The northern branch of the Chicago and Northwestern Railroad transverses some of the wealthiest suburbs in America including Wilmette, Winnetka, Glencoe, Highland Park and Lake Forest. Though these suburbs are as economically exclusive as they are appealing, people are still finding old houses that have been neglected and are undervalued. Incredibly, every so often someone finds an old house in the North Shore or far western suburbs so neglected that the electrical wiring predates World War II.

Outside of Chicago the area of greatest renovation activity is the "inner belt" suburbs of Oak Park and Evanston. Evanston, world famous as the home of Northwestern University and the Women's Christian Temperance Union, is a genteel and venerable Victorian suburb immediately north of Chicago. In the early 1970s harbingers of blight became evident in Evanston — empty and boarded-up stores, houses in disrepair and slumping building values. Evanston's leadership did not ignore these warning signs and undertook corrective action, such as encouraging commercial redevelopment of the central business district and providing financial aid to low and moderate income home owners for building code corrections (anyone desiring more information about Evanston's home owner's aid program should contact the Evanston Department of Housing and Rehabilitation in the Evanston Municipal Building). The village's efforts to reverse decay has thus far been successful, and building values are again rising. The areas of Evanston with the greatest potential for renovators are the central section west of the Northwestern Railroad and east of Ridge Boulevard, and the southeastern section west and north of Calvary Cemetery.

Oak Park is the land of Wright, and consequently, an architectural mecca. It was Frank Lloyd Wright and Louis Sullivan, Wright's mentor, in fact, who led American architecture out of the European-dominated Victorian era, and many of Wright's greatest works are in Oak Park. Nevertheless, in the early 1970s Oak Park found itself facing urban blight. Neighboring Austin of Chicago had recently undergone rapid racial change and was just as rapidly becoming a

slum. Signs became manifest that Oak Park would soon follow —
banks redlined the suburb, real estate brokers steered whites to one
area and blacks to another, and white families began to flee southeast Oak Park. To halt incipient blight, Oak Park took bold action
including moving the village hall to the vulnerable southeast neighborhood and converting the village's main business street into a mall.
Thus far, Oak Park's community renewal programs have been successful, but building values, especially in southeast Oak Park, have
not yet caught up with other western suburbs, and hence present an
opportunity for renovators optimistic about Oak Park's revival.

This attractively-ornamented wood-frame house clearly needs a coat of paint. The other repairs it might need are more difficult to spot.

3

Evaluating the Condition of Old Houses

Old houses in blighted neighborhoods almost invariably require major repairs. Searching in such neighborhoods for unrenovated buildings still in nearly perfect condition is probably a waste of time. One should aim not so much at finding a house in good condition as at making an accurate estimate of necessary repairs before buying the house. Knowing the condition of a building enables a prospective buyer to estimate whether he can afford the building, to negotiate intelligently with the seller, and to avoid unforeseen costs. Nothing will turn a renovation into a nightmare faster than the discovery that thousands of dollars must be spent immediately for an unanticipated repair.

Because an accurate assessment of a building's condition is so important, many buyers arrange for a professional inspection, at a cost usually of $50 to $150. It's worth the expense, if for nothing more than peace of mind. Architects and contractors who specialize in old building renovation often inspect buildings for people who have not contracted for their complete services. There are also professional building inspectors whose sole livelihood is the inspection

57

of buildings. They are listed in the yellow pages under "Building Inspection Service." It is preferable that the inspector be a registered engineer, but if he is experienced with old residences and has a good business reputation, it is not absolutely necessary. The inspector should provide a written report that includes an evaluation of the building's basic systems and structural integrity, an estimate of repair cost, and recommendations for repair.

A professional evaluation becomes even more crucial if a buyer intends to make extensive changes in the building's interior. Some changes cannot be made within a reasonable budget, and some cannot be made at all. One common alteration, for example, is removing an interior wall to create more space. A simple partition can easily be removed, but more than a few architects and contractors can tell horror stories about clients who, without consultation, set about removing a load-bearing wall. Anyone considering a building renovation should make sure his plans are practical before he purchases.

In many old houses a cursory examination will reveal the need for new plumbing, wiring, heating, and some structural repair. People who buy houses in such disrepair anticipate large renovation expenses and usually compensate by purchasing at little more than the value of the land. However, houses that need no structural repair or new service systems are usually much more expensive, and an unexpected repair in them can be deadly to the renovator's budget. To avoid this, many provident buyers call in specialists to help them estimate expensive repairs such as reroofing a tile roof or rebuilding a blocked fireplace chimney. Contractors in these specialized fields will often make inspections at a nominal charge, usually $25 to $50.

If possible, the buyer should go along on the inspection so that he can ask questions and discuss various approaches to renovation and repair. To ask intelligent questions and to be sure that the house is thoroughly inspected, the buyer should have inspected the house beforehand on his own. When inspecting an old building, wear old clothes. Old buildings are often dirty, and the dirtiest places are usually the ones that require the most inspection. A penknife, a flashlight, a screwdriver, a marble, a magnet and a ladder will be useful. If a ladder is inconvenient, binoculars can be used instead. The inspection can start at the top and work down or at the bottom and work up, but it must be systematic and thorough. This review inspection will begin at the top.

ROOFS

Pitched Roofs —

If the roof is covered with asphalt roll, look for rips, cracks, or patches. Asphalt roll usually lasts only ten to fifteen years.

If the roof is asphalt shingle, look for missing shingles, broken shingles or shingles that have rolled up at the corners. An asphalt shingle roof should last fifteen to twenty years.

If the roof is clay tile, glazed tile or slate shingle, look for cracked, broken or missing tiles or shingles. A tile or slate roof properly maintained should last thirty years or more, and some slate and tile roofs in the Chicago area have lasted nearly one hundred years. The felt roofing paper under the tile or slate, however, needs to be replaced every thirty years on average. Reroofing or repairing a slate or tile roof is far more expensive than similar work with asphalt shingle or roll roofing. If there is any question about the condition of the roof, it would be wise to have an expert examine it.

Look for depressions in the roof planes or sags in the roof ridge. Depressions or sagging may signal broken or rotting roof joists.

Flat Roofs —

(Be careful about walking around on a flat roof. Sharp heels may crack it.)

Look for depressions in the roof. Depressions may indicate trouble with a roof joist or roof board and water may have penetrated into the interior. A poorly draining roof will allow water to stand, and freezing and thawing water will quickly destroy the roof.

Look for cracks or bulges. Cracks often allow interior water damage, and bulges may soon become cracks.

Check the flashing along exterior walls, chimneys and roof openings such as trapdoors or skylights. If flashing has pulled away from a wall or opening, water may have gotten under the roof covering to cause interior damage.

Check the capstones on top of exterior masonry walls. A cracked or missing capstone could indicate serious interior damage, including structural deterioration.

Check metal cornices and gutters. Small areas of metal erosion can usually be repaired inexpensively with asphalt roofing compounds or fiberglass. However, if large sections of metal have corroded and rusted away, the cost of repair will be high.

CHIMNEYS

Check for sound masonry. Large masonry chimneys often deteriorate and have to be rebuilt.

If the chimney cap is cracked, broken, or missing, the masonry may be damaged.

EXTERIOR WALLS

Check the caulking around all windows and doors and the flashing above windows and doors. If the flashing or caulk has been broached by water, there could be interior damage.

Sills should be sloped away from the window and free of rot. If they are not, serious interior damage may have occurred.

Check for cracks in the outer walls and in the foundation. Cracks may have been caused by settling, which usually isn't a problem, or they may betray more serious structural damage. If there is any doubt about what caused the cracks, a professional should examine them before the building is purchased.

Check doors for proper alignment in their frames. Doors out of alignment may indicate serious structural problems.

Check around the foundation. Earth should slope away from the building and downspouts should be attached properly to the downspout shoe. If water has been allowed to stand near the foundation, it may have drained into the basement.

Check that earth has not been piled above or against any wood in the exterior wall or foundation. Damp earth can cause rot or damage from termites or carpenter ants. It would be best if gravel was around the foundation, as it allows for drainage and prevents capillary action.

Check brickwork and foundations under porches. This is an area that is often neglected.

Check the condition and size of the windows. Windows in many old houses are not a standard size. Replacement sash will have to be custom ordered from a millwork, so it will be more expensive than standard mass-produced sash. Storm windows will have to be custom-made for old houses with windows in non-standard sizes, at about twice the cost of standard stock storm windows.

Masonry stained by running water from defective gutters cannot be restored except by replacing the damaged bricks. This is difficult, expensive, and, if matching brick cannot be located, impossible.

If mortar has weathered or leached out, water will enter the wall and cause damage. Such a wall must be retuckpointed.

If masonry walls are vine-covered, check carefully under the vines. Ivy tends to attack mortar, and the vines may have to be pulled down so that the masonry can be retuckpointed.

Painted masonry presents a problem and a risk. There is no way of determining the masonry's condition until after the building is purchased and the paint stripped. If the brick is badly marred or unattractive, it will have to be repainted, a task that will have to be repeated every five to seven years.

If the bricks are pitted or spalled, their original appearance cannot be restored. All an owner can do is apply a sealant to the masonry to prevent any further deterioration.

Sandstone and some soft limestone spall and corrode. Restoring deteriorated sandstone and limestone facades is difficult and not always successful. It is best to have an expert examine decayed or damaged sandstone or limestone before purchasing the building.

Most wood-clad houses have been covered with a false siding. There is no way of knowing the condition of the underlying wood clapboards without removing the siding — they may be rotting, they may be nearly perfect, or they may have been removed altogether.

If the house has original clapboards, check carefully where the clapboards join the end boards. Often the clapboards will pull away from the end boards because of aging and shrinkage, allowing water to enter the walls.

Cracks or small bulges in the clapboards can usually be repaired, but long lengths of warped board will have to be replaced.

If the paint is weathered, repainting will present an immediate and major expense.

ATTIC

Look for water or water marks on roof boards that may indicate a leak in the roof.

If moisture is condensed on the roof boards or if mildew is growing there, the attic is either inadequately ventilated or in need of an insulation vapor barrier. As long as no rot has developed, both problems are easily rectified.

Check for insulation between the attic floor joists. If the attic is not insulated, insulation should be a high-priority expenditure, at a minimum of several hundred dollars. Old houses with flat roofs often do not have an attic or even a crawl space between ceiling and roof. To properly insulate such a house may require tearing apart the ceiling, a fairly large expense.

FLOORS

Check for sagging or tilt. A marble will roll down the slightest incline, so use a marble if you are unsure about floor level. Uneven floors may result from no more than uneven settling (a certain amount of which is almost inevitable in old houses) but they may also indicate structural damage. Check the ceiling below the floor. If it sags as well, damaged floor joists are probably to blame. Replacing floor joists is messy and expensive, since to get at the joists the ceiling below must be torn down. First-floor flooring is usually easier to repair because basements usually have no ceiling. In any case, get a professional opinion.

Floors in old houses are often covered with several layers of linoleum or carpeting, making it impossible to determine the condition of the floor or even the kind of wood. However, in some old houses there are still registers in the floor from old gravity-air furnaces. If the register can be lifted up, the kind of wood can sometimes be discerned from the crosscut around the register opening. Hardwood is a definite plus.

If the floor is loose or gives when walked on, the cause could be a broken or loose floor joist, or nothing more than a loose floor plank. Replacing or repairing a loose floor plank is generally simple and inexpensive. Another possible cause is a lack of bridging between floor joists, since some nineteenth-century builders did not bother to use this kind of bracing. Check the first-floor joists in the basement for joist bridging. The lack of bridging may be an annoyance, but it is not generally serious.

Check floors in bathrooms, kitchens and anywhere else that water damage may have occurred. Constant exposure to water can cause wood to rot or turn black. Usually black discoloration from water is too deep to be sanded out, and the flooring will have to be replaced.

Check bathroom floors for bounce. In many old houses floor joists were notched to accommodate new plumbing pipes. Such notch-weakened joists will have to be repaired or replaced.

STAIRCASES

If the staircase sags or if risers and trends have pulled away from the stringers, the staircase may have to be rebuilt — usually at considerable expense. Missing balusters are relatively inexpensive to replace if they are softwood in a simple turned shape. However, hardwood balusters with intricate designs can cost from $20 to $100 apiece to replace.

FIREPLACES

Check the draft by lighting a small piece of paper and observing whether smoke rises in the chimney (be sure the damper is open). A poor draft or no draft at all may result from an inadequate smoke chamber or firebox and can usually be corrected with a ventilator. However, if the flues have collapsed, the chimney will have to be opened and rebuilt — a very expensive repair. If there are any doubts about the condition of a fireplace or chimney, consult an expert.

If a chimney is unlined and there is evidence of deteriorated mortar joints, such as spalled mortar in the ash dump, it may be wise to have the flue lined.

Missing or broken tiles around the mantel are usually easy to replace with imported Mexican tiles available from most tile retailers.

INTERIOR WALLS AND CEILINGS

Check walls and ceilings for wetness or watermarks. Damage on or near exterior walls may indicate that the outside walls have been broached by water. Ceiling or high wall damage from water on the top floor of a house usually results from roof leaks. Ceiling or wall damage from water on lower floors usually means faulty plumbing.

Plaster should be attached firmly to wood lath. It should not be crumbly. Small cracks and holes can be repaired if the surrounding plaster is undamaged.

When checking the condition of walls and ceilings, consider whether the building requires a major rewiring or replumbing job. If it does, many of the walls and ceilings will have to be torn apart and rebuilt regardless of their condition.

As with exterior walls, large vertical cracks may indicate structural damage. Have an expert examine cracks to be sure of the building's structural integrity.

BASEMENT OR CELLAR

Dampness is the bedevilment of cellars. Look for signs of water penetration such as flood marks on the basement walls or damp spots around girder posts or under stairs. There should be no standing or running water on the cellar floor.

Check all wood members — foundation sills, floor joists, girders, girder posts — for rot. Use a knife or screwdriver to penetrate the wood. The wood should be firm, and it should not break off into chunks.

Efflorescence on foundation walls could indicate past flooding or a slow seepage of water from outside.

PLUMBING

Check basement plumbing lines for the kind and condition of their metal. Ideally, water lines are copper or brass and waste pipes are a thick-walled cast-iron. Use a magnet to determine whether the pipes are galvanized iron (iron is magnetic, copper is not). Galvanized iron lines do not last as long as copper. Use a knife or screwdriver to check for lead pipes. Lead is soft and will scratch easily. Lead pipes will have to be replaced. Check the waste lines by striking them with a metal object. If the pipe is thick-walled, it will make a dead, stonelike clank; if the pipe is thin-walled, it will have a metallic ring. Thin-walled waste pipes do not last as long as thick-walled pipe, and replacement of waste lines is expensive.

Check the pipes for leaks, especially around joints.

Check water pressure by turning on all the faucets on a single line at the same time and observing whether pressure is noticeably reduced, especially in the bathroom after the toilet is flushed. Pressure problems are usually caused by pipes that are either too small or are plugged with scale or sediment.

ELECTRICAL WIRING

If room lights are turned on by a pull chain or by the old two-button switches, count upon a major rewiring job, as the electrical system is probably obsolete.

Check the panel board (it probably is in the cellar). The panel board should have its amperage rating clearly marked. Air-conditioners and kitchen appliances will require 150 to 200 amps. If three wires enter the panel box, the house is wired for 240 volts; if only two wires enter the box, the house is wired for only 120 volts.

Consider the kind of heating and cooling systems to be used in the house. New electric space heaters, heat pumps, or central air-conditioning will require the installation of new service lines, at an expense of a thousand dollars or more.

HEATING

Most old buildings were heated originally either by hot water, steam or warm air. If the furnace is an old coal burner that has been converted to oil or gas, it may have to be replaced. Such furnaces are often fuel-inefficient. If the house has a doubtful looking boiler, get a professional inspection. A new one will cost between $3,000 and $8,000.

Installation of a forced-air heating system in a steam or hot water heated house will require ductwork in the walls and ceilings. The cost of wall and ceiling repair after this work should be included in the estimate for a new heating system. Since many boilers serve as hot water heaters, if a forced-air system is to be installed, a separate hot water heater will have to be purchased as well.

Incredible as it may seem, it is not uncommon for people to buy old houses without ever once stepping inside. When a building reaches a certain stage of dilapidation, especially in a depressed neighborhood, one no longer looks for what might be wrong with the building, but rather assumes that everything is wrong. With this approach to building renovation, later surprises can only be pleasant: anticipated repairs sometimes turn out to be unnecessary, and money is saved, not spent. Of course, the condition of the building will be reflected in its selling price. When a house sells for $5,000, one can assume without ever inspecting the structure for water marks on the plaster or sagging stairways that the cost of making the building habitable will be many times the selling price. Buildings that sell for less than $20,000 usually require more than $40,000 to be made habitable again. When one is renovating on such a scale, an underestimation of $5,000 to $10,000 may disappoint a renovator, but it will not ruin him.

People spend large sums of money to renovate badly dilapidated buildings in the belief that the money will be returned in increased building equity as the neighborhood redevelops. Several of the McCormick Seminary townhouses were purchased without inspection, but the buyers were able to base their estimates for repair on previously renovated townhouses, and they were confident that the increasing value of the townhouses would cover any rehabilitation expense. But for the most part, building values escalate rapidly only in redeveloping neighborhoods. Unexpected costs for rehabilitating a deteriorated house in a stable neighborhood may not be recovered in increased building value. Therefore, it is more important for a buyer to be sure about repair costs for a slightly neglected or even recently renovated old house in a stable neighborhood than for a badly deteriorated house in a depressed but redeveloping neighborhood.

One last consideration about inspecting old houses. Many old houses are completely habitable, yet lack their original attractive appearance and interior amenities. From ignorance or lack of taste, previous owners of old houses often made abominable alterations, from bricking up fireplaces and lowering ceilings to replacing oak front doors with cheap flush doors. The cost to restore the original appearance and features of such abused houses often far exceeds the rehabilitation costs. Therefore, anyone who buys a habitable but demeaned old house should be very clear about the cost of restoring the building to its original elegance.

4

Purchasing and Financing the House

Buying a house is often a trying experience. There may be a war of nerves with the owner during the price bargaining. If more than one person is interested in a house, there is anxiety over bidding — optimally, the winning bid will be greater than all others but by very little. If a sale is agreed upon, there is no assurance that financing will be available. Financial institutions will not offer a mortgage until a Sale Contract has been signed, but no one wants to spend the time and effort trying to buy a building only to discover financing is unavailable.

Buying an old house can be even more trying, for financing arrangements are often more complex, and financing availability more limited. Savings and Loans frequently refuse mortgages on old buildings that do not meet Building Codes. Of course few unrenovated old buildings still conform to Building Codes, forcing potential buyers to seek financing elsewhere. Financing may be even more difficult to obtain if the old building is located in an area deemed risky by financial institutions.

Red-lining is the practice, or alleged practice, by financial institutions of denying home purchase or building repair loans in a specific geographic area. Loan decisions are based not on the credit-worthiness of the applicant or the condition of the structure but rather on the location of the building. The effect of this geographic discrimination, it is charged, is to cause money-starved areas to deteriorate.

Financial institutions of course deny they red-line. Yet there is no dearth of witnesses who claim they experienced or witnessed financial red-lining. Long-time Lincoln Park residents can recall how potential buyers were forced to look elsewhere because financial institutions would not loan them money. Of course now Lincoln Park is the hottest and safest real estate market in Chicago. When the restoration of Pullman began in earnest in the late 1960s, home buyers could get financing for no longer than a 9-year term. As the restoration movement gained momentum, financing arrangements improved to 12-year terms by 1970 and 15-year terms by 1972. With public criticism and scrutiny, financial institutions seem to red-line less frequently, at least less conspicuously. But anyone trying to buy an old house in a neighborhood still blighted may find financing difficult to find or terms, such as down payment or repayment period, less favorable than desired.

The first step in purchasing a building after an inspection is determining whether you can afford it. Are the costs to purchase, renovate and maintain the building within your means? To determine this, costs should be separated into *immediate* and *continuing* expenses. Immediate expenses include the loan down payment, lawyer fees, title insurance and search fees, recording fees, mortgage closing costs, service charges or points, and immediate non-delayable building repairs. Continuing expenses include monthly mortgage payments, real estate taxes, renovation loan payments and general operating costs (water and sewer charges, heating, insurance and utilities).

IMMEDIATE EXPENSES

People buying a house often feel like the Sabines during the Roman plunder — raped. Everyone seems to grab for the buyer's money. The financial institution, which would seem adequately remunerated by interest on the loan, also charges for appraisals, credit checks and "interest in advance," or points, and closing costs. In Chicago, there is a transfer tax of a penny per ten dollars on building purchases (for example, a building purchased for $100,000 will be taxed at $100). In addition, most buyers hire a lawyer before buying a building. In all, an immediate expenditure of a thousand to several thousand dollars may be required at the time of closing.

The standard down payment demanded by financial institutions in recent years has been twenty percent. (For example, on a building selling for $40,000, a financial institution would provide only $32,000 with the buyer making up the $8,000 difference.) However, in old blighted neighborhoods financial institutions often demand twenty-five to forty percent down, and if the building needs immediate repair, the financial institution may condition a loan on the buyer (or seller) making the immediate repairs. Buying a house in a still-blighted neighborhood may require more immediate cash expenditure than a comparable building in a redeveloped neighborhood, although the purchase price is usually significantly lower.

The immediate outlay to buy an old house, for down-payment and sundry closing costs, averages twenty-five percent of the purchase price. (For example, an old house selling for $40,000 would require at least $10,000 for immediate expenses.) But anyone buying an unrenovated old house should be prepared to spend more for non-delayable repairs. Certain repairs, such as leaking pipes or a damaged boiler in winter, cannot be delayed until bank financing is obtained, if it can be obtained. The buyer of an old unrenovated building should have a cash reserve for contingencies.

CONTINUING EXPENSES

The largest single continuing expense is generally the monthly mortgage payment. However, in older blighted neighborhoods it is not uncommon for a building's renovation costs to exceed the purchase cost. A building costing less than $20,000 to purchase will usually require that much and more to rehabilitate. During the first several years with such a house, renovation costs, whether interim financing or out-of-pocket outlays, are usually greater than the mortgage payments.

Real estate taxes are a continuing expense payable in Cook County yearly or in installments. Real estate taxes are determined by applying a tax rate to a building's assessed valuation. The tax rate, set by local government, escalated sharply in the 1960s but has remained fairly constant during the 1970s and has actually decreased in Chicago. It is the assessed valuation that causes real estate taxes to rise so precipitously. The Cook County Assessor reassesses the fair market value of every building in the county every four years, and if the neighborhood has redeveloped, tax bills will increase as building values increase. Low-income residents of redeveloped neighborhoods are more often forced out by higher taxes than by unban renewal bulldozers.

Besides real estate taxes, every building has a continual operating expense, including costs for heating, water and sewer, insurance, electricity and, perhaps, natural gas. If the building is poorly insulated, the heating bill might be reduced after insulation is installed. The remaining operating costs are not likely to be reduced and, on the contrary, will probably increase with inflation. Operating expenses can be estimated from past expenditures. Real estate agencies usually list such information right on a building's sales sheet, and a buyer can demand that the building owner provide his past bills for heating, electricity, taxes, etc.

DETERMINING A BUILDING'S AFFORDABILITY

To purchase an old house, then, a person must be able to afford both the immediate and the continuing expenses. But if the estimated immediate expenses exceed a person's cash reserves, he still has several options. He can look for another, less expensive building, perhaps in a neighborhood in earlier stages of redevelopment. People wanting an old house often set their sights on the finest streets of Lincoln Park when they should be looking in Lake View, Logan Square or Wicker Park before these areas also become expensive. Or he can choose not to buy immediately but to bide his time, saving money and hoping mortgage costs will decrease (when mortgage money isn't tight, points and closing costs are often lowered). This is a gamble based on the hope that savings will increase and immediate expenses decrease faster than building prices will increase. A final option is to convert or borrow money on some other less liquid asset, such as a life insurance policy or stock. However, anyone trying to budget a building purchase to the penny is taking a risky gamble. Most people renovating in Chicago have underestimated renovation expenses.

Whether a buyer can afford the continuing expense of a given building is more difficult to determine, since future incomes and expenses can only be estimated. The standard guide to housing affordability has traditionally been that a home owner should pay no more than 25 percent of his take-home pay on housing. During the first several years of a renovation building owners often spend fifty percent of their take-home pay on housing, but this is a temporary sacrifice. However, if heating costs, taxes and mortgage payments exceed 25 percent of net pay, in the long run the building will probably prove unaffordable. A buyer should be cautious about very spacious old houses, especially masonry-constructed buildings. Large houses often have large heating bills and masonry constructed buildings are particularly difficult to insulate.

Real estate taxes often become the most onerous continuing expense. An old dilapidated building usually carries a small real estate tax, but following rehabilitation it is reassessed and taxed more heavily, especially in old but exclusive suburbs. The only reprieve from taxes a building owner can expect is the Home Improvement Exemption, instituted in Cook County in 1975. This exempts a building from increased valuation for four years, as long as renovating expenses do not exceed $15,000.

THE BUILDING PURCHASE

If a building seems affordable, the buyer begins the process, or ordeal, of purchasing.

A building buyer is not required to have a lawyer by law, but it is chancy for a layman to buy a building without one. Real estate transactions are complicated and the risks great. An attorney specializing in residential real estate can be located through the Chicago Bar Association referral plan. The initial consultation with the Bar-referred attorney costs $10, and of course there is no obligation to retain the lawyer. In recent years law clinics, staffed by young lawyers and offering reduced fees for simple real estate closings, have sprung up throughout the city. The price is right, but a buyer should be sure that the lawyer is capable. Old buildings are often tax delinquent, in housing court, or have liens or covenants on the title of which the buyer must be aware. Most people buying an old house locate an attorney by referral from a friend or associate who had a previous successful transaction with one. This is probably the wisest approach.

The extent to which a building's selling price is negotiable depends upon whether it is in a "buyer's" or "seller's" market. In popular neighborhoods, such as Old Town, DePaul or the Gold Coast, a building for sale usually attracts several interested buyers. Unless a building owner has grossly overestimated the value of his property, the selling price is usually pretty close to the asking price. It is not uncommon for a bid to exceed the asking price when several people are bidding for the same property. However, in blighted areas buildings often remain for sale for many months, allowing a buyer more negotiating leverage. If a building has been for sale for more than six months without generating any interest, the owner may have to admit that his asking price is too high and accept the lower counter-offer. In view of the considerable risks in buying a dilapidated building in a blighted neighborhood, it is advisable for a buyer to try to bargain an asking price down by biding his time, even though by waiting he chances losing the building to another buyer.

Once the buyer and seller have agreed upon the building's selling price, a Real Estate Sale Contract is signed. The Sale Contract is provided by the building owner's agent, either his lawyer or his real estate broker. Usually it is a standard form supplied by a real estate board or title insurance company. Whatever the form, Sale Contracts consist of the same general terms and conditions. As with purchase price, most terms in the Sale Contract will be agreed upon before the Sale Contract is signed.

The provisions covered in a typical Sale Contract are:

1. Of course, the agreed upon building purchase price.

2. A legal description of the real estate.

3. An enumeration of personal property included in the sale, particularly property attached to the building, such as carpeting, stoves, refrigerators, drapes, chandeliers, water softeners, etc. Failure to include such an enumeration can lead to disputes as to whether the

property may be taken by the seller, or whether it passes with the building to the buyer. Be sure that everything wanted and agreed upon as part of the sale is listed in the contract.

4. An enumeration of conditions on the property, such as taxes due, easements, leases, agreements (such as party wall rights), special assessments due, liens, etc. The buyer should be sure he does not become liable for taxes or special assessments he has not agreed to.

5. A specified amount of earnest money, paid at the signing of the Sale Contract or at a specified time immediately thereafter. Earnest money is a guarantee to the building seller that the buyer is seriously trying to purchase his property. If the buyer should fail to comply with the contract, the earnest money is forfeited to the seller for his time and expense. Until the purchase is completed, the earnest money is usually held in escrow or by the seller. Eventually it is used as part of the down payment. In some real estate transactions earnest money may be placed in escrow even before the Sale Contract is signed.

6. The particular financing arrangements and a specified length of time to obtain financing. The buyer might take over a mortgage already on the building or seek a new loan from a financial institution or combine the two, as the contract specifies. Usually there is a time limit to obtain financing, with a clause returning the earnest money to the buyer if financing cannot be obtained and the owner or his agent is so notified. Be sure the contract specifies financing terms — interest rates, repayment periods, total loan amount. Otherwise the seller can make a binding offer to provide the financing himself at terms favorable to him and adverse to the buyer.

7. The date and the place of closing.

8. The date purchaser takes possession will be specified, with a clause

that the seller will pay rent if the date of possession falls after the purchaser becomes legal owner.

9. The designation of an agent to hold the earnest money. (Usually the real estate broker or the seller's lawyer.)

10. A condition that the seller assure that there is no legal problem with the title to the property. This is usually done through the seller obtaining, before the closing, a commitment from a title insurance company to insure the title to the property.

On standard Sale Contracts there are usually a number of other conditions, such as requiring the owner to cooperate with financial institutions assessing the property for loan purposes, or to maintain the property and provide access. If these conditions are not already in the contract, they should be included here.

When agreement has been reached on all provisions in the contract, it is signed and becomes binding. As noted earlier, it is only after a Sale Contract has been signed that financial institutions will consider formal application for a home mortgage commitment. Nonetheless, a preliminary search for financing should have been conducted. Financial institutions may not provide a commitment for financing before a Sale Contract has been signed, but they will usually communicate their loan conditions — interest rate, length of repayment term, down payment requirement, service charge, closing cost charge and general availability of loan funds.

The extent and intensity of the search for financing depends upon the general credit market. If the credit market is favorable, the search is for the best deal. A little money might be saved if a Savings and Loan Association is found with a slightly smaller interest rate or service charge. However, if the credit market is extremely tight, as it was several times during the 1970s, the financing quest may be a frenzied search for any deal, much less a good one. During a favorable period a credit-worthy buyer should be able to procure financing at most Savings and Loan Associations. In a tight market period, however, a buyer's chances are better in a Savings and Loan where he or a close relative has an account or has borrowed before.

As noted earlier, the Sale Contract will specify an agreed-upon length of time for the buyer to obtain financing. At the first possible opportunity after the Sale Contract has been signed the buyer should apply for a mortgage loan at a Savings and Loan Association that gave a prior indication of financing availability. It would seem sensible to apply at several Savings and Loan Associations simultaneously to increase the likelihood of receiving a loan commitment. However, financial institutions don't like spending time and money processing a mortgage loan application only to discover that the applicant has accepted a commitment from a rival institution. Savings and Loan Associations in Chicago dislike this practice so much that many insert a clause in the application prohibiting the applicant from applying elsewhere at the same time, and make an effort to eliminate anyone making multiple applications.

Actually it should not be necessary to apply to more than one Savings and Loan. If the credit market is good, anyone credit-worthy should be able to locate a financial institution optimistic about a loan commitment even before application is made. If a person should be rejected for a home purchase loan for no discernible reason (credit-worthiness, tight money market) except red-lining, there is a program in Chicago that allows an applicant to appeal to a public review board — the Home Mortgage Opportunity Committee of Chicagoland (HMOCC). To attempt redress, apply for appeal at any member Savings and Loan Association and they will dispatch the appeal to the review board, or send the appeal to HMOCC, P.O. Box 516, Chicago, Illinois 60690. The program is too new to assess, but such review board programs have met with little success in other cities where red-lining is an issue because there have rarely been any appeals to the appeal board.

After a check of the applicant's credit-worthiness and an appraisal of the building being purchased, the Savings and Loan Association decides whether or not to extend a financing commitment. The loan terms will be dependent upon market conditions. During a favorable period terms are generally twenty percent down payment, 8½ to 9 percent interest, on a twenty year repayment schedule with 1½ to 2 points for conventional self-amortizing mortgages. (A self-amortizing loan is a self-liquidating loan that repays the principal and total aggregate interest in constant monthly payments over the duration of the repayment term.) During tight money periods, interest may be nearly 10 percent with points of 2½ or 3.

There are other forms of home purchase financing, such as balloon mortgages and contract buying. A balloon mortgage is not self-amortizing; that is, the borrower makes payments only to cover interest and then at the end of the mortgage term (usually one to five years) the principal is paid in one lump sum. The danger of balloon mortgages is of course in not having sufficient funds to repay the principal, or balloon, at the end of the mortgage term and being forced into foreclosure. Still, balloon financing has been used successfully by renovators in Eastern cities who were denied conventional self-amortizing financing by bankers skeptical of a neighborhood's chances of redeveloping. As the neighborhood does redevelop and the value of the renovated building appreciates, the owner-renovator can refinance and pay off his balloon mortgage.

Contract financing is a method of finance used mainly by low-income building buyers not credit-worthy enough for conventional mortgages. It is a method prone to abuse by unscrupulous businessmen who evict contract buyers who miss a payment. Such a practice was an element of plot in Upton Sinclair's *The Jungle*. Still another finance method is the "take-back" or purchase money mortgage, where the building owner will offer to finance the home purchase himself by terms enumerated in the Sale Contract. There are also private companies and brokers that offer mortgage financing. While each of these financing methods has advantages and drawbacks, the predominant and preferred financing method for middle- and upper-income building purchasers in Chicago is the conventional self- amortizing mortgage loan from local Savings and Loan Associations or banks.

When money is tight, obtaining financing to buy a house is difficult enough, but if the house is in serious disrepair, obtaining financing may be next to impossible. Savings and Loan Associations do not like committing money on buildings not in conformance with City Building Codes. It is common practice, in fact, for Savings and Loans to demand a Certificate of Conformance (provided by the Building Department or a private inspector through a building inspection) before granting a loan. Savings and Loans reason that if the buyer fails to rehabilitate the building and goes into default, then they are stuck with a building that may be unmarketable.

However, during favorable money periods when Savings and Loan Associations sometimes have savings deposits sitting idle, they tend to be more flexible in loan requirements. They may increase the purchase loan to cover renovation expenses if the buyer will increase his equity. For example, if a $40,000 building is purchased with a 75 percent home loan ($30,000) and the buyer puts an additional $5,000 of his money into the building's repair, then the Savings and Loan will provide 75 percent of the increased equity ($3,750) for further renovation. The advantages of this financing arrangement is that the buyer has to deal with only one financial institution and terms are usually the most favorable possible since the increased financing is still part of a first mortgage. The disadvantage, clearly, is that it puts an additional burden on the buyer's cash resources at a time when immediate expenses are already high. As often as not, a buyer will have to turn to a bank for interim financing to buy and rehabilitate a dilapidated building.

Banks will provide financing to buy and renovate dilapidated buildings, but usually with stringent requirements. First, banks usually offer only short term financing, which is far more expensive than long-term financing. If the renovation takes longer than expected, the financing cost may bankrupt the owner. Secondly, banks often make loans contingent upon the buyer first obtaining a commitment from a Savings and Loan for a mortgage on successful completion of the rehabilitation. The bank's rationale is that, even if the building is renovated, if the owner can't get a mortgage to repay the short term loan, the bank must foreclose. For the buyer this means dealing with two financial institutions simultaneously, each with its own requirements and restrictions. Third, some banks won't provide financing if the owner intends to do some major repair work himself. They fear the owner will make a muddle of the renovation, not repay the loan, and leave the bank with an unmarketable building. The bank may even want the applicant to have already contracted a reputable architect and/or general contractor before it grants a loan. Yet many people must use some of their own labor, from financial necessity or because contractors refuse to take the job (see Chapter Six). Thus the buyer is caught in a Catch-22 trap. No one ever said buying and renovating an old house was easy.

Once a building is purchased, there are other means to finance repairs. One of the most prevalent methods of repair financing in America is Title 1 loans. Title 1 loans, one of many FHA (Federal Housing Administration) housing programs, are available through most financial institutions (Savings and Loan Associations, banks, credit unions, mortgage companies, etc.). Terms for Title 1 loans are 12 year repayment at 12 percent interest on a $10,000 maximum loan. While Title 1 loans are generally easy to obtain since they are Government guaranteed, there are conditions on them that might be adverse to the owner doing restoration work himself. For example, one qualification is that the borrower live in his house for at least 90 days. For someone buying a house in need of immediate attention, a three-month residency may simply not be practical. In this case, conventional financing is the only option.

Other methods to finance a renovation include Home Improvement loans and second mortgages. A Home Improvement loan is a personal credit loan and is not secured by a mortgage. It is a bank loan intended, as its name suggests, for home improvement — enclosing a porch, remodeling a kitchen or bathroom, putting on new paint or siding, etc. In type, the Home Improvement loan is similar to an auto purchase loan — a short term loan, rarely over $5,000, with from 10 to 15 percent interest depending upon the general money market.

Another approach to renovation financing is a second mortgage. A second mortgage is similar to a first mortgage — the financial institution lends money to a homeowner and places a lien or claim on the property — except that the holder of the first mortgage has primacy over the property if it is foreclosed. Since a second mortgage carries more risk for the lender, the interest rate and monthly payments are greater for the borrower. A second mortgage, therefore, is generally not as desirable as refinancing a first mortgage. However, for renovators in blighted areas, a second mortgage may be one of the few financing options avaliable. After the renovation has been completed and if the neighborhood does redevelop, the building owner can usually combine or refinance all his debts into one first mortgage.

While most home purchases and renovations are financed through private financial institutions by conventional means, there are a number of government programs that may be of some interest to the middle-income owner-renovator. Government funding in the urban renewal program, for example, played a major role in abetting private renovation in Lincoln Park and Hyde Park. Myriad programs exist, administered by myriad government agencies. They include programs administered by the Federal Housing Administration (FHA), the Veterans Administration (VA), the Model Cities Program, the Department of Planning, and the Department of Housing and Urban Development.

The housing programs of the Federal Housing Administration date back to the Great Depression. The FHA is an expression of the Government's belief that every American should be able to own his own castle. In fact, FHA programs were instrumental in providing Americans with homes during the post-war housing boom of the 1950s and 1960s. However, by the 1970s the Federal Housing Administration had come under assault for acquiescing in the deterioration of inner city neighborhoods.

Under most FHA and VA financing programs, the Federal Government guarantees repayment of any FHA-approved home purchase or home repair loan, and since Government backing eliminates an element of risk, the financial institution can offer better terms — lower down payments with low monthly mortgage payments (because the loan repayment period is longer). Thus, thanks to FHA backing, a person with small cash savings and low income can afford to purchase a house. While a low down-payment and low monthly mortgage payments may be alluring, most middle- and upper-income buyers opt for conventional financing instead. FHA and VA insured loans have several disadvantages — the FHA must approve the contractor and may limit the amount of work the building owner does himself. In addition, FHA loan programs are targeted mainly for code compliance repair work and may not be compatible with an old house restoration.

One government renewal program that may be of interest to lower-income property owners is the Financial Assistance to Property Owners Program of the Department of Planning, City and Community Development. An owner-occupant of a building of from one to four units can receive a grant of up to $15,000 per unit from the Financial Assistance Program for major repair work depending upon the owner's income and family size. The smaller a person's income and the larger his family size the more money he can receive from the Financial Assistance to Property Owners Program. This program is obviously a very attractive program as the City is giving the building owner money to repair his property. However, the Program's eligibility requirements eliminate most people interested in buying and renovating an older building. For those people earning less than $12,000 a year who are interested in the Financial Assistance to Property Owners Program, more information can be obtained at the Rehabilitation office of the Department of Planning, City and Community Development, 205 W. Wacker Drive.

A Government program of more interest to higher-income building owners is the 312 Loan Program (from Section 312 of the Housing Act of 1964).

The 312 program is a loan program with financing provided directly from the Federal Department of Housing and Urban Development. Building owners in urban renewal areas who need financing to bring their buildings into Building Code compliance can receive a loan up to $27,000 at three percent interest and with twenty years to repay. Considering that most renovation financing carries interest rates of from eight to eighteen percent, a loan for three percent is rather attractive. Of course, as with all Government programs, there are drawbacks, such as bidding for contractors rather than negotiating. But the greatest drawback is the program's funding uncertainty. The 312 Loan program has had a checkered existence. Under Republican Presidents the program was barely funded at all. With a Democrat President funding has been more generous but still full of vagaries. One year Chicago is allocated more than a million dollars for 312 loans, the next year substantially less than a million. Consequently, there may not be financing available for all eligible applicants. It would be wise to check the availability of 312 financing before buying a dilapidated old building with the hope of obtaining a 312 loan. The 312 Loan program is administered by the Department of Planning, City and Community Development, 205 W. Wacker Drive.

The aforementioned Government housing programs are by no means the only ones. There are others, such as the Urban Homestead Program of the Department of Housing and Urban Development, which is an effort to rectify some of the carnage caused by the FHA in the inner city, and the Chicago Home Purchase and Rehabilitation Plan, sponsored by the Model Cities Program and a group of Chicago Savings and Loan Associations to assist creditworthy individuals in purchasing a home in several designated inner city neighborhoods. These programs offer no benefits to middle- and upper-income old house buyers.

Those Government programs of interest to middle-income old house buyers suffer the same deficiency as the 312 Loan program — inadequate funding. Chicago's low-interest mortgage program (called the "Chicago Plan") introduced in June of 1978 and copied by several suburbs, including Oak Park and Evanston, is an excellent program that can save a home buyer $50 a month or more on his monthly mortgage payment. (The City sells tax-free municipal bonds to lend money to Savings and Loans, who then lend the money to home buyers at lower than market interest.) However, despite the infusion of hundreds of millions of Government dollars, only a few thousand mortgages are funded — a small number in comparison to mortgages funded conventionally. Still, it might be wise to check with a participating Savings and Loan Association, such as First Federal of Chicago, about a low-interest "Chicago Plan" mortgage before seeking a conventional mortgage.

This apparently modern building is actually a renovated Victorian.

5

Renovation, Rehabilitation, Restoration and Preservation

The words *renovation, preservation,* and *restoration* are often used interchangeably, as if they are synonymous. They are not, though even architects, planners and designers frequently use them as such. Understanding their differences introduces an issue important to anyone renovating an old house — how a house should be renovated to maximize its value, and how residents can maintain the quality of life in their neighborhood.

The building pictured opposite is a three-story brick, painted white with contrasting dark-tinted windows, in obvious modern style. While the building may appear to be of modern construction, it is actually a renovated Victorian. Renovation has a rather broad definition, meaning simply to bring back to a good or useable condition. This is the definition of rehabilitation, also.

Renovating or rehabilitating an old building, then, may mean nothing more than repairing any deterioration and improving basic service systems. At the other extreme, it may mean redesigning and restructuring the entire building, interior and exterior, as in this example.

89

Whether this particular renovated building is attractive or not is of course a matter of personal taste. The owner-renovator explained his choice as follows:

> This house appealed to me for several reasons. It was an in-nocuous house, a neglected house — a house that was not built with the beauty with which many of the row houses were con-structed. A little ticky-tacky house. I didn't like the idea of dese-crating something that was beautiful. It would have broken my heart to strip down a beautiful house, but this was a simple rec-tangular shell. (Quoted in *How to Buy and Remodel the Older House,* by Cobb, page 434.)

It is true that the building was not especially distinguished, but neither was it "a simple rectangular shell." It was a handsome struc-ture with embellished lintels and a cornice with decorative brackets, similar to many on the north side of Chicago which are quite attrac-tive when restored to their original appearance. The total redesign of an old building can be done only if the owner believes that the building's original appearance is not worth conserving. The reno-vator in this example redesigned his building because it lacked dis-tinctive beauty, not because it was abominable. Not everyone takes Victorian architecture so lightly. Recently increasing numbers of people have come to believe that old buildings should be preserved or restored rather than redesigned.

Preserving a building means retaining, with slight repair, a struc-ture that is essentially in its original condition and appearance. Pres-ervation is the saving of a past that still exists. After decades of neg-lect and indifference, few old neighborhoods in Chicago have build-ings in their original condition and appearance. Most old buildings in Chicago must first be restored before they can be preserved. Res-toration is a more specific form of renovation or rehabilitation — it is bringing back a building as nearly to its original appearance and condition as is practical. Restoring a typically dilapidated old house can be a herculean task, but the result is usually worth the effort. There have been several recent building restorations in Chicago, right down to cast-iron stoves in the kitchen and china fixtures in the washrooms, that are inexpressibly beautiful.

Since nineteenth-century buildings were gas illuminated, coal heated and without electricity, a true and faithful restoration is not practical or sensible. A museum is not a home. Neither are total restorations always economically feasible. Too often old buildings are so badly stripped that restoration becomes prohibitively expensive. Sometimes it is not possible even to determine what the structure's original state was. One woman whose North Side brownstone had been stripped of everything except the original staircase was able to restore the building only because she had the building's original architectural drawings.

While a true restoration is impractical due to financial constraints and the need for modern conveniences, the intent to restore as much as possible bespeaks a respect for the building not shared by the "gut to a shell and redesign" renovator or rehabber. This new respect for old buildings is the result of a changing consciousness in America. Previously, anything new was held to be desirable and anything old equally undesirable. Those people who did remain in older buildings felt compelled to make their older homes at least look new. In the early 1960s, after the City of Chicago proposed that Pullman be demolished and replaced by industry, concerned residents tried to dramatize their commitment to the community by "modernizing" their row houses. With false siding, aluminum awnings and large picture windows, Pullman residents tried to make their nineteenth-century Queen Anne rowhouses look like twentieth-century suburban townhouses. Still, the community was spared the wrecker's ball.

When renovation of old buildings did become fashionable, it was often done with no more reverence for the building's original character than had been the case with the "modernizations." Renovators or rehabbers used old buildings to express their own creativity. Old buildings were something to be made chic and unconventional. Plaster was stripped from brick walls which were then sandblasted and left bare; floors and walls were torn out, creating large open spaces for a cathedral effect; roofs were broached for large central skylights, and exterior facades were given whole new window treatments. Whatever the building had been, it was no more.

Once a building has been redesigned it is virtually impossible to restore, and with each redesign or demolition original nineteenth-century buildings become increasingly scarce. The old maxim tells us that nothing is ever really appreciated until it is gone, and the changing attitude toward older houses was perhaps caused in part by the realization that they would soon be gone if attitudes did not change. In recent years older urban dwellings have come to be appreciated for their original character. High plaster ceilings are not something to be hidden with false acoustical tile ceilings; natural wood floors are not something to be covered with linoleum; paint does not belong on natural woodwork or marble fireplaces and siding with phony designs cannot improve an original facade. What is old is no longer scorned because it is old; it is instead appreciated for its intrinsic charm. And more and more, renovations are done as restorations.

While renovations that respect a building's integrity have gained currency in recent years, there is still a minority who view old buildings as objects to be refashioned. Because just one ill-considered and conspicuous exterior redesign can detract from an entire block or neighborhood, public movements have grown to limit the rights of property owners to alter their building's appearance. When the McCormick Seminary townhouses were sold into private ownership, organizers attached restrictive covenants to the row house title deeds, preventing owners from altering their building facades.

In established neighborhoods, the effort to regulate property owners has been by landmark designation. A neighborhood can become a landmark district only after the City Council has enacted a designation ordinance upon the recommendation of the Commission on Chicago Historical and Architectural Landmarks citing the area's "special historical, community, or aesthetic interest or value." Once an area has been designated a landmark district, property owners are prevented from either demolishing their building or altering its appearance without the Commission's approbation. Though landmark designation does pre-empt some traditional property rights, most residents in Chicago's landmark districts feel that the reward is worth this sacrifice. Besides assuring neighborhood preservation, the prestigious designation and the publicity it creates has increased property values. The past is being preserved for the future to the betterment of the present.

Landmark designation is an important legal tool for preserving the architectural character of old neighborhoods in Chicago, but it has several drawbacks. In scope and application, landmark designation is limited to "special" neighborhoods and not all old neighborhoods in Chicago worth preserving are eligible. And even if all old neighborhoods were eligible, landmark designation is not always effective. In Mid-North, Old Town and Astor Street, where real estate developers were demolishing old dwellings to construct larger, more profitable buildings, landmark status has thus far been a salvation. But in neighborhoods where redevelopment is just beginning, large areas of land lie fallow from prior building demolition. When these neighborhoods regenerate, if they do, new construction will fill the vacant land, yet there is no legal mechanism preventing new development from debasing the architectural character of the neighborhood. New construction, radically different from existing buildings in size, mass, set-back, color or building material, can be more damaging to a neighborhood's architectural character than altering the appearance of existing structures. Still the Landmark Commission's position thus far has been that guildelines, much less restrictions for new construction, are "neither feasible nor desirable."

Government regulation and restriction of new development in old neighborhoods is neither new or radical. In other cities restrictions protecting old neighborhoods were employed long ago. In Georgetown, new development must conform to certain restrictions, including a 90-foot height limit, and be approved by the Washington Fine Arts Commission. In Savannah, new buildings must meet established design criteria before approval. In Boston, San Francisco and other enlightened cities, there are also established safeguards for neighborhood preservation. Chicago, as usual, has taken longer to address the problem. In 1964 the Urban Renewal Department commissioned a survey and study of neighborhood preservation prior to the Lincoln Park Urban Renewal Project. The study, entitled "Preserving the Architectural Character of a Neighborhood," recommended design criteria for new development and rehabilitation and outlined various legal safeguards for preserving the character of old neighborhoods. Yet as the 1980s approach, the study's recommendation — "To prevent disharmonious and unsuitable developments, new legal tools forged to achieve aesthetic control, must be examined and tested" — has not been achieved.

Landmark designation, land use planning, zoning codes, building codes are not esoteric parlor games for bureaucrats and lawyers. They have a very real and profound effect on the quality of life and property values in old neighborhoods. Some people in old neighborhoods found that the Zoning Ordinance did not allow rehabilitation of multi-unit buildings. If the zoning designation was upgraded, allowing renovation of deteriorated apartment buildings, then developers could build new apartment buildings, causing rent increases, traffic congestion and parking shortages. Other building owners suddenly found themselves in the shadow of a new high-rise, reducing their quality of life and the value of their property.

Anyone buying an old house must vigilantly protect his investment and quality of life, since he has little protection in Chicago's ordinances. An individual has little power to effect change, but when individuals form or join community organizations, their power is greatly increased. Community organizations have, for instance, successfully changed their neighborhood's zoning designation to prevent the proliferation of high-rises. Other groups have lobbied successfully for tavern prohibitions in residential areas and for Building Code amendments to eliminate cheap, jerry-built multi-unit apartment buildings. Anyone who buys a house in a redeveloping old neighborhood without taking an interest in how the neighborhood redevelops may be at the mercy of people interested only in a quick profit.

A building owner who hopes to maximize the value of his rehabilitated building should be aware that the chic redesigned buildings of the Sixties are no longer selling as well as authentic Victorian houses. People now want more than a rectangular shell with one large window.

6

The Renovation — Preliminaries

The first priority of any renovation must be to secure the building physically from thieves and vandals. Though violent crime in redeveloping old neighborhoods is relatively rare, property crime is not. Renovators are a favorite target of burglars looking for easily fenced power tools, stereos, televisions, etc. Vacant or abandoned buildings are particularly vulnerable. Rip-off artists often cruise through old neighborhoods looking for buildings that might contain such valuable and easily purloined objects as stained-glass windows, chandeliers, copper pipes, even hardwood doors.

There is no failsafe security system against the professional burglar. Some building owners have spent thousands of dollars for sophisticated electronic security systems only to be burglarized repeatedly. But most burglars in redeveloping neighborhoods are easily deterred juveniles, and the best deterrent is simply to make the house look lived-in by putting up curtains or blinds. If a house is not going to be occupied during the renovation, it might be wise to remove stained-glass and any other valuable fixtures until the building is occupied. (Police in Chicago and some suburbs will on request evaluate a building's security. In Chicago, for a police inspection call the Preventive Program Division.) With the house secure, the renovation can proceed.

The next priority is to arrest the spread of deterioration and prevent its recurrence. If your building has a leaking and rotting roof, it will be foolhardy not to begin the renovation with the roof repair. Similarly, it would not be wise to ignore an unreliable heating system at the outset of winter, for if the plumbing lines should freeze and rupture, a far greater expense will be incurred than for heating repair alone.

DOING THE RENOVATION YOURSELF

Once the building is safe from vandalism and further deterioration, a considered decision must be made as to how much of the renovation work you, the owner, will do yourself. For people of moderate means, providing some labor themselves will be a matter of financial necessity. Not everyone can afford the luxury of paying someone else to strip paint from woodwork, sand floors or patch plaster. But for those with financial flexibility, how and by whom the building is renovated is strictly a matter of personal choice. There is a certain breed of building renovator for whom restoring an old building is an avocation, perhaps even an obsession. To him, the caution, "This repair can be done only by a skilled craftsman," is a red-flag challenge. The more difficult the task, the more satisfying the repair. On the other hand, some people have no taste whatsoever for getting paint in their hair or grit under their fingernails. You should be honest with yourself about this.

Personal inclinations aside, whether you renovate your house yourself or retain professional labor depends in part upon the condition of the building. If your building is structurally sound and you have decided against a major building redesign, you can almost certainly muddle through much of the repair yourself. But when a building needs major structural repair, such as replacing weakened load-bearing walls or floor joists, you will have no choice but to obtain professional help. A building structurally deteriorated is likely already to have been inspected by the Building Department and found in violation of the Building Codes. As the Building Codes of Chicago allow only registered architects and structural engineers to submit drawings for approval of structural work and prohibit anyone but a certified professional from doing electrical or plumbing work, you would have to contract professionals to remain within the law even if you had the desire and ability to do the work yourself.

But except for those areas legally restricted to professionals, there are really few repairs the average houseowner cannot undertake. In neighborhoods where building renovation is rife, on sunny warm weekends whole blocks are astir with people working on their buildings — painting, repairing gutters, tuckpointing walls, etc. Perhaps the best restraint on what repair work you should attempt is your own common sense. As a criterion for deciding whether to try a repair or not, consider what the worst conceivable consequence of a botched repair could be in damage and cost. For example, tuckpointing masonry is a laborious task but not particularly difficult. Generally anyone with some troweling and striking tools, rented scaffolding and pre-mix mortar can successfully tuckpoint a wall. And if you do manage to bungle the job, you are not likely to cause any other damage. On the other hand, the consequences of a bollixed plumbing repair can be severe water damage, and a bungled electrical repair can cause a devastating fire.

Even seemingly straightforward repairs can sometimes be devastating. One renovator with a first floor sagging because of weakened floor joists decided to repair the floor by putting a steel beam perpendicular to the joists. The weight of the floor would thus be carried by the beam supported by two steel jack posts. The renovator was even savvy enough to know that the concrete basement floor would not support the concentrated weight of the first floor transmitted through the posts. So he broke through the concrete and set two new post footings. Unfortunately one of the footings was placed over an old pipe that collapsed under the new burden, and the sud-

den shifting of weight caused plaster to crack and fall throughout
the building. The repair procedure was sound, up to a point. The
renovator simply had not considered all possible contingencies.

In deciding whether to attempt a particular repair, you should
consider the consequences to your person as well as to your property.
Recovering a roof, even repairing a rotted roof board, is not overly
difficult for an amateur. But a steep roof is a dangerous place to work,
even for a professional. Still, with a little foresight, a little luck, and
a lot of common sense, most self-repair work can be accomplished
without disaster.

If you want to do your own repairs but you lack experience or
expertise, advice can be had from several sources. First, you can seek
the services of a professional inspector. The necessary repairs and
how they should be made should have been discussed with an inspector at the time of the initial inspection. But as the renovation progresses, new questions may arise and if you were satisfied with the
inspector's knowledge (and fee) you could employ him again to review the provisional repair plans. The fee for professional advice may
be a good investment if it prevents a larger expenditure to rectify
mistakes.

Another way an amateur can acquire some professional expertise is to employ and observe a professional as he completes part of
the job. For example, if a house needs extensive plaster repair, you
can employ a professional to repair part of the structure, such as the
first floor, observe how the repair is accomplished, and then complete
the work yourself. You can always decide to retain the professional
if finishing the repair yourself seems too difficult or unpleasant. The
disadvantage is that hiring professionals in this piecemeal fashion
may be more expensive than hiring them for a complete job. Still,
piecemeal hiring may allow you to discover and fire an incompetent
worker before he damages the entire house, and in this case the additional expense may be worthwhile.

Another way to acquire knowledge about renovating old houses is by conferring with owners of similar buildings who have already completed a rehabilitation. In sections of Lincoln Park, Lake View and Wicker Park, for instance, entire blocks of buildings were built by the same developer and will have much in common. To meet other owner-renovators in the area, inquire with local block clubs and neighborhood or community organizations (list in appendix). Most renovators will be happy to share their knowledge and experience with you.

There is one universally applicable piece of advice for renovators: always plan ahead before commencing work. Once an action has been taken, it may not be easy to rectify. To decide in retrospect that a room would have looked better if walls had not been removed or plaster sandblasted down to brick is futile, for the damage can be undone only at great expense. Similarly, it is heartbreaking to discover that a ceiling painstakingly replastered and restored must be torn down to insulate the attic or repair a weakened joist. Poor planning can cost as much in anguish as it does in money.

Planning is essential. Yet it must also be said that strict adherence to a plan is not always possible. You cannot fully anticipate the unknown no matter how provident you try to be, and even if the building was given a thorough inspection before its purchase, you will likely make discoveries after the renovation has begun that will interfere with the original plan. For example, one renovator discovered that the full-length mahogany sliding doors he expected to restore had been sealed shut because the previous owner had used the slide space for electrical conduit. To make the doors functional again he had to reroute the electrical wiring. Of course not all new discoveries about a building are going to be unfortunate. There may be parquet floors under the hideous linoleum.

People who have renovated their own houses often recommend living in the building for a time, if possible, before starting any major work. This gives you an opportunity to learn more about what repairs will be needed, and it gives you a feel for such things as the proper size of rooms and their most convenient uses. Many renovators immediately open up large spaces and move bathrooms and kitchens to different locations, both expensive changes. You might well decide, after living in the building for awhile, that there is a good deal to be said for the original design. At any rate, it is best not to rush into the renovation (except for damage that requires immediate attention) and to know the house well before making any major decisions.

If you do plan to live in the building during the renovation, you should provide yourself with at least some comfortable living space, preferably in the uppermost part of the house. Renovations typically require one or more years to complete, which is a long time to live under unpleasant conditions. If just one room in the house is reasonably pleasant, it can be an escape from the frustrations of a decayed building. Renovating a house is a dirty process, which is why it is best to start from the top and work down. Besides the general accumulated dust and dirt of an unkept old house, tearing up plaster ceilings and walls or sanding floors constantly generates new dust and detritus. By living in the upper part of the building, at least the benefit of gravity is gained. Nevertheless, air-borne dust will settle even in the upper living quarters, so it is best to store as many possessions as possible somewhere else until the renovation is complete. Those possessions that must be kept in the house during the renovation should be covered with plastic sheets. One renovator bought and installed a new washer and drier before starting the renovation to insure a ready supply of clean clothes. Several other renovators suggest purchasing a highpowered industrial vacuum cleaner for removing sawdust, plaster dust, etc., faster and more effectively.

ARCHITECT-ADMINISTERED RENOVATIONS

If the rigors of an extensive do-it-yourself project are not for you, and the house you have chosen is in serious disrepair, you may need the services of an architect. The best time to choose an architect is even before a house has been purchased, so that he can help you evaluate the building's condition and estimate renovation costs. If you like his proposals and can afford them, he can begin drawing up construction documents as soon as the building is purchased. If, on the other hand, you find that for one reason or another the architect does not suit the job, at this point all he is entitled to is a fee for his time as a building inspector. You should be sure you have a good rapport with your architect before engaging him to do much work. Otherwise, terminating the relationship may be costly.

The first phase of an architect-administered renovation is often called the design phase. At this stage, besides evaluating the condition of the structure, the architect may draw some preliminary sketches or perspectives, interior and exterior, of how the building will look when completed. Architects enjoy drawing up these perspectives, and they can help people to evaluate alternatives in the use of space and in building appearance. But unless the interior is going to be radically altered or the exterior restoration will be extensive, perspectives may not be absolutely necessary. Often the architect's real work begins with the preparation of the construction documents.

The construction documents, which include the floor plans and building specifications, are the comprehensive instructions for the building's rehabilitation. It is the architect's responsibility to see that the construction documents are accurate, complete and in conformity with the Building Codes. For many laymen, architectural drawings might just as well be Chinese, and building specs can addle the mind. Nevertheless, you should try to muddle through them and gain some understanding. Among other things, the building specifications enumerate the materials to be used in the renovation, often by brand name. If these are not the materials you want, the time to change the plans is before the work has begun.

Contractors prefer bidding on jobs defined and controlled by architect-prepared construction documents, for they provide the contractor with a greater degree of certainty as to what the renovation entails. The more uncertainty there is in a job, the more likely contractors will bid high for their own protection. No contractor wants to get stuck in a contract that will ultimately cost him money. Architect-prepared construction documents may save you some money, if they prevent contractors from padding their bids to be on the safe side. Besides providing construction documents for contractor bidding, the architect should act as an advisor to his client during the bidding. An architect familiar with renovation should know if the contractors' bids are reasonable or not, and so counsel his client.

In addition to aiding in contract bidding, the architect's construction documents, or at least his floor plans, are often a legal necessity. Any renovation that entails more than ". . . minor repairs to maintain existing parts of a building" will require a Building Permit from the Chicago Building Department. And if work is going to be done to any load-bearing element of the building — a roof beam, exterior wall, girders, for examples — then an architect or structural engineer must submit four sets of floor plans to the Building Department to obtain a Permit. Most suburban municipalities have similarly stringent permit requirements. More will be said about Building Permits and what an owner can do himself later in this chapter. For now, it is enough to say that if the renovation is being conducted by an architect, it is generally his responsibility to obtain a permit, though sometimes contract documents will specify that the contractor is to obtain the permit.

After the general contractor and subcontractors have been chosen and the building permits procured, the actual work can begin. It is the responsibility of the contractor and the subcontractors to execute all their work in conformity with the construction documents and Building Codes, and the architect should see to it that all work is so done. Architects do not want to be held responsible for the inadequacies or irresponsibilities of contractors, so they often play down their supervisory obligations. While an architect should not be held

to blame when contractors violate their contracts, still he must supervise the renovation, no matter what he prefers to call this job: overseeing, watchdogging, advising, whatever. In many renovations the
most important role the architect will perform is seeing to it that
work is executed properly by tradesmen. Design work is important,
but in many renovations the bulk of the design effort was done by
the Victorian architect a century before. What an owner of an old
building requires in an architect is someone who will oversee the
construction as if he, the architect, were going to live in the building
afterwards. The architect may have been engaged in the first place
because the owner lacked the technical expertise to assure that the
renovation would be done properly. You as building owner must
rely on the architect to safeguard your interests. If you are considering using an architect, try to determine beforehand whether he diligently monitors the unglamorous, mundane but crucial construction work.

An architect who specializes in old building renovations, if he is
to do justice to his client and the building, must be able to control
his own desire to express his creativity. An architect, after all, is a
cross between an artist and an engineer. For an architect designing
new buildings, the only real limitations to his creative expression are
the client's needs, tastes, and budget. But an architect renovating a
fine old house ought to be limited by the design of the original building. Unfortunately, many old neighborhoods are disfigured by buildings that were renovated by architects with more ego than sensitivity.
In recent years, perhaps because public attitudes in favor of preserving original exteriors have become so prevalent, few architects dare
to redesign an old facade. Building owners still find, however, that
some architects have a basic disregard for the charm and character
of original Victorian interiors. One house owner reports that his
architect recommended replacing an original Victorian mantel with
a large, thick plate of glass, so people could watch "the flames danc-
ing up the fireplace."

Architects, like lawyers and doctors, do not advertise their services and fees, so if you want an architect who specializes in old building renovation, you will have to search for one. (Actually, young architects are beginning to advertise in such publications as *The Reader*.) As short a time as a decade ago, it was difficult to locate architects who knew much about house renovation. But with growing interest in renovating or recycling old buildings, more and more young architects have turned to renovation as a specialty. The Chicago Chapter of the American Institute of Architects, located in the Glessner House, has a referral list of member architects who specialize in historic restoration. Historic restoration is of course a very specific type of renovation. If you own a building in the landmark class, you may find that an architect knowledgeable in historic restoration will best fill the project's needs. However, most people renovating an old house simply need a competent architect who will respect the original character of the house, and there are many of these in Chicago.

The best place to look for architects specializing in building renovation is in neighborhoods where renovation is current. Several neighborhood organizations (list in appendix) in redeveloping areas maintain a referral list that includes architects who have performed satisfactorily before. Architects often work mainly in one community where they achieve a local reputation (which could be good or infamous, of course). The officers and staff of neighborhood organizations are generally aware of who these architects are. Also, general contractors who specialize in building renovation are often familiar with architects in their field, as they may have worked with several. Have a look at some renovations in progress. If the contractor is destroying the charm and character of an old house, any architect he recommends is likely to share the same disrespect. On the other hand, if the contractor possesses a solicitude for old houses, architects he recommends likely will as well.

Another way to find out what kind of work a particular architect does is to ask him for references to previous clients. Naturally, most architects will refer prospective clients to the past work of which they are most proud. Looking at this work should tell you whether the architect prefers to do major interior redesigns of the "chic" variety or adaptive renovations that retain much of the original design while filling the needs of a modern family.

On the other hand, you might learn a great deal more about an architect by talking to clients who have ended up in litigation with him rather than with those who praise him. Perhaps a better way to determine an architect's ability is to work backwards — look for exemplary renovation work, then find out who the architect was. One way to inspect renovated houses in redeveloping neighborhoods is to go on the periodic walks and open houses that neighborhood organizations sponsor as fund-raising projects to promote the neighborhood. If a house seems to be exceptionally well renovated, ask the owner whether he used an architect and if so whether he was satisfied with the architect's service. Or you can inquire for an architect through real estate agencies. Renovated houses are always on the market for sale, and real estate agents who have worked in a redeveloping area for a long time usually know which architects do the best work.

Many renovations in size and nature simply do not require the full services of an architect. It is not necessary to hire an architect to conduct the complete renovation if only particular architectural services are required. Architect's services and fees can be arranged in several different ways. They can be paid at an hourly rate, by negotiated fee and schedule, or by a percentage of the renovation cost. For example, an architect might agree to provide a client with architectural drawings and specifications for a flat fee, payable when the documents are delivered, and then "watchdog" construction work for another flat fee, payable when construction is successfully completed. Some architects will work at an hourly rate — so many hours to inspect a building, so many hours to draw plans, etc. A client should get a reasonable estimate of how many hours the architect will require to complete the task properly and keep track of the architect's time on the job. In addition, architects are sometimes employed for a combination of hourly and flat fees for different segments of the renovation.

If the renovation is a big and expensive project, the architect is usually paid a percentage fee, usually between ten and twenty percent depending upon the size of the project. Not many architects will be interested in a percentage arrangement for full services if the total renovation costs less than $20,000. It simply would not pay. Architects retained with a percentage contract usually are paid on a prearranged schedule — ten percent of fee after inspecting the building and drafting perspectives, thirty-five percent of fee after drawing floor plans, seventy-five percent of fee after construction documents are completed, eighty percent after contractor bidding is completed, and one hundred percent paid after the renovation is completed. Generally, in percentage contracts an architect is required to complete the renovation within ten percent of the agreed-upon total cost. If he fails to do so, he may be required to pay the difference, though this depends on the specific terms of the contract.

When Chicago-area renovators express dissatisfaction with an architect, they generally complain either that the architect was more concerned with cosmetics than with the practicalities of the renovation, or that he was negligent in overseeing construction. If you are satisfied with the physical layout and interior features of your old house and want only to upgrade the building's service systems, you want an architect who is more interested in building engineering than in interior design. When architects slight the utilitarian needs of a house for the decorative trappings, the result is often a house that fails to provide basic comfort. In one case, an architect failed to give proper attention to the design of a new forced-air heating system, and the result was a house uncomfortably hot in one area while uncomfortably cold in another.

But the single most frequent shortcoming of architects has been their failure to oversee construction work properly. Even when building owners are willing to pay the architect an hourly rate to inspect ongoing construction, too often he is impossible to locate when he is needed most. One house owner whose architect was too often a phantom found that the general contractor had put two return air ducts and no warm air duct in one room and had put a toilet in the wrong location in a new bathroom. The consequence to the owner was additional expense and more time lost. A sad reality of building renovation is that when contractors do their work wrong, contractual obligations to the contrary, the house owner often pays part or all of the expense to rectify these mistakes.

If you feel you must depend upon an architect to administer your renovation, make every effort to determine that he will renovate the house to your tastes and style of life, not his own, and that he will protect you diligently from contractors' blunders.

GENERAL CONTRACTORS

There are general contractors who rehabilitate old buildings, and then there are general contractors who desecrate old buildings. Irresponsible contractors have done more than their share of despoiling the urban landscape in old neighborhoods. These entrepreneurs gull whole blocks into having the cornices torn off their houses because "they're only going to deteriorate anyway," or into buying false siding "to make the old house look new again." Just because a general contractor is certified to do building repair work in Chicago does not mean he is capable of renovating an old house. As with architects, if you are considering a general contractor, be sure that he has an appreciation and respect for the integrity of old buildings. Otherwise, he is likely to cause irreparable harm.

An architect designs and directs the renovation, but the general contractor brings the design to reality. The general contractor does

Planning a renovation or estimating cost is difficult because there is
no way of knowing beforehand what might be found behind walls
or under paint. The wallboard behind the stove in the photo above
might have concealed an unpleasant surprise such as damaged
plumbing lines. In fact it hid a pair of hardwood doors
in nearly perfect condition (opposite).

all the actual work, structural repair, plumbing, electrical rewiring, installing new heating and air-conditioning systems, new plastering or sheetrock, bathrooms and kitchen remodeling — everything necessary to rehabilitate the building. The general contractor employs or subcontracts the laborers and craftsmen, purchases the building material and acquires all necessary permits. If you as building owner have contracted a responsible general contractor, you have relieved yourself of locating all the subcontractors and tradesmen necessary to renovate a badly deteriorated old house. Furthermore, if time is an important factor, as it may be if you cannot live in the house until it is rehabilitated or if a bank loan is contingent upon a construction deadline, an experienced and responsible general contractor can usually complete a renovation far quicker than you can.

As the conquences, financially and emotionally, of contracting an unqualified or derelict general contractor can be so great, make certain that the contractor you choose is reputable and qualified before entering into any contractual arrangement. Old building renovation is a specialty that requires unique abilities. A contractor whose bailiwick is enclosing front porches, converting basements into rec rooms or building attached garages does not possess the expertise to renovate old houses. As with architects, the best measure of a general contractor's ability is his past work. When you see an old house that has been properly and tastefully renovated, find out who the general contractor was, if one was used. General contractors often place prominent signs on buildings they are renovating to promote new business. Observing a general contractor as he works should provide some insight into his ability, as will talking to the owner of the building. If you have ever retained an architect knowledgeable in renovation, contact him for recommendations. He will probably know several qualified general contractors worth considering.

The critical information to garner about a general contractor is, did he try to follow the intent of the contract and building specifications, or did he fulfill only their barest surface meaning? If a general contractor is conscientious, he will strive to be sure that the work done is really what the client wants. No matter how detailed and explicit the contract and building specifications might be, instructions can often be interpreted in more than one way, and unforeseen situations can easily arise. When questions come up, does the general contractor try to communicate with his client or his client's architect? Or does he do the job perfunctorily, without any real concern for his client's well-being? A good general contractor will consider the interests of his client even beyond contractual obligations. As the work progresses, he will watch for new ways in which his client might be benefitted, such as by saving material costs or anticipating future problems.

Even when you have found a general contractor you feel you can rely on, for your own protection insist on a detailed and comprehensive construction contract. If it is not in the contract, it is not legally binding. The contract must be detailed in regard to responsibilities, procedures and payments. The building materials you want must be specified in the contract. If you want yellow tile in the bathroom, the contract must specify yellow tile. If you want a certain brand of forced-air gas furnace, that furnace must be specified in the contract by manufacturer and brand name. The architect's specifications are important at this point, for they can be incorporated into the contract and made binding. If you are not using an architect, you yourself must provide building specifications. Otherwise you risk the loss of legal recourse if work is not done as you desire.

To protect yourself in contract negotiations with a general contractor, you as owner must either be conversant with building renovation and contract law or retain a lawyer for legal counsel. If you were satisfied with the lawyer who guided you through all the legalities and pitfalls of purchasing your building, you should probably retain him for all remaining renovation contracts and legalities.

A contract with a general contractor must be fair to both contractor and building owner. Each side will want as many contract safeguards to protect his interests as possible, and each side has a right to some guarantees. A house owner may require the general contractor to provide a performance bond insuring that work will be completed as specified in the contract. And the general contractor may require the house owner to place in escrow with a trustee the contractor's future remuneration. After all, just as building owners try to protect themselves from irresponsible general contractors, so general contractors try to protect themselves from derelict clients. A house owner who intends to pay for his building renovation with vague hopes of a bank loan or a lucky day at Arlington Park is not a good business risk.

General contractors will seek to get the bulk of their payment in the early stages of work and before construction actually begins. A general contractor is entitled to some advance payment as he does have start-up expenses, such as workman's compensation insurance and building materials. But as building owner, you should seek a payment schedule with the bulk of the payment during the later stages of the renovation and upon its completion, for the withholding of payment is your greatest leverage. You can always threaten to sue if a contractor violates his contract, but litigation is slow and costly. The best means to persuade a general contractor to rectify his mistakes is to threaten to make no more payments. (As a further safeguard to assure that the general contractor is complying with the contract, you should reserve the right to examine all bills paid by the general contractor for building supplies. And as a protection against nuisance liens, you should demand a waiver of lien from any subcontractors used, when payment for completed work is made.) If time is vital you may desire a completion deadline with a penalty clause. If so, the general contractor will probably want a clause exculpating him from contingencies over which he has no control, such as a labor strike that holds up necessary building supplies or bad weather that precludes exterior work.

Besides all the preceding contract considerations, you and the general contractor will need to agree upon an amendment procedure for contract changes. In addition, you should be sure the contractor has adequate workman's compensation insurance, and that you yourself have adequate home owner's liability insurance.

The established practice for selecting a general contractor and determining his compensation is by competitive bid. Several general contractors, rarely more than three, are invited to bid on the renovation after inspecting the house, studying the construction documents and conferring with the owner. Following bidding, the general contractor with the lowest bid generally — but not always — gets the job. Government loan programs administered by the Department of Urban Renewal require advertise-and-bid competition. This arrangement theoretically assures a house owner of paying the least amount possible. Nevertheless, one should be very careful in accepting a low bid, especially if it is much lower than the others. A general contractor can reduce his profit only so far, and controlling costs by working efficiently has its limits. Some contractors can get better deals on materials than others, often by ordering in quantity. Even so, the building specs place a limit on how much can be saved on materials, since a given product finally has a rock-bottom price. More than likely, a low-bidding contractor has underestimated the renovation cost. Once the project begins and he realizes he is going to lose a lot of money, he will want to renegotiate the contract, or, as often happens, he will walk away from the job, reasoning that bankruptcy will come faster by completing the job than by litigating a civil lawsuit.

Although competitive bidding for general contractors is still a common and approved method of selection, it is becoming just as common for people to negiotiate a contract with a single general contractor. The possible additional cost of several thousand dollars is acceptable to these people if it enables them to secure a general contractor whom they feel is honest, competent and solicitous of their building's character. Whether you select a general contractor

by direct negotiation or by competitive bid, you should already have
a good idea of what the job will cost. If nothing else, you should have
gotten a reasonably accurate cost estimate from an inspector before
purchasing the building.

For a building rehabilitation project to be financially worthwhile
to a full service general contractor, it must be big enough to employ
his total crew. Such general contractors will not be interested in a
renovation that only requires some upgrading or remodeling. For
smaller projects, a building owner is better off doing his own contracting or repair work.

Besides requiring enough work, general contractors usually avoid
jobs that may involve uncertainties in cost or time. This is another
problem for the person trying to restore an old house. A general contractor can make a reasonably accurate estimate of what it will cost
to demolish an interior, install new service systems and rebuild walls,
ceilings and floors, because in essence he is building a whole new
building inside the walls of an old one. He can control construction
costs through his labor scheduling in a gut and rebuild renovation;
when one tradesman is done working, another can begin. However,
if an owner wants his house repaired and remodeled while leaving
the bulk of the interior unchanged, the general contractor is left unsure as to how long it will take or how much it will cost. If one repair requires more time than expected, he may end up with the rest
of his crew idle and his costs escalating. The sad reality is that it is
easier to tear out an old interior than to save it. Thus, many people
in Chicago who have wanted to preserve and restore the original
interior features of their old house have discovered that no reputable
general contractor would bid on the job, forcing the owner to subcontract or do the work himself. General contractors will sometimes
offer to accept a restoration on the basis of a "cost-plus" contract. In
a cost-plus arrangement the general contractor is paid whatever his
cost to repair the house is, plus an agreed-upon profit. This type of
open-ended contract can be perilous, since you have no idea what

the renovation will cost until the general contractor presents the final bill. Most people familiar with building renovation warn never to get involved in an open-ended contract unless you have complete confidence in the integrity of the contractor.

SUBCONTRACTING

For a variety of reasons — a sense of personal accomplishment, the inability to raise necessary financing, a desire to minimize labor costs, a renovation too small or too difficult to interest a general contractor — many people choose to do their own general contracting and some manual labor themselves. Whether by choice or necessity, if you are going to direct your own renovation you must possess a knowledge of what the renovation entails. You must know what you want and be resolute in getting it. The building owner must command the workmen he employs, never the other way around. The scourge of building renovation is workmen who cause more harm to a building than existed before the repair.

Nearly every house owner who has undertaken a renovation has a repertoire of horror stories about careless workmen. One man renovating an old house in Lake View came home one day to discover that workmen had thrown his antique French windows in the garbage. A murder might have ensued had not the windows been rescued from the refuse. Another house owner had a marble vanity ruined when a workman tried gluing the marble to a wall and the glue soaked through, staining the marble. Unfortunately, a prior reputation for competent work does not guarantee that the workmen will continue to perform in the same fashion. One resident of Old Town hired a building contractor, on the community's list of recommended tradesmen, to rebuild his deteriorated back porch. Halfway through the job the builder disappeared and was never seen again. A much beleaguered house owner on the Near West Side hired an architect of good repute in the neighborhood to admininster his house rehabilitation. With the renovation only a third completed, the architect decided computers offered a more promising future and quit architecture. The house owner found an architectural firm of two young architects to assume the original contract. Shortly thereafter the two architects had a business disagreement and dissolved their partnership. The house owner found a third architect to complete the renovation but would have been better off if he hadn't. The architect failed to oversee construction work adequately and much of it was done wrong.

Just because someone puts a shingle over an office and places a phone number in the yellow pages does not mean he is really competent. One enterprising individual was claiming to be a "third-generation" carpenter when actually he had learned carpentry several years before in a Park District craft shop. Working on old houses requires a special talent — patience. The owner of one very old but charming house had three carpenters walk off the job before he found one with the patience and ability to complete the renovation. The house had a slight lean and a floor badly out of level, which is not unusual for old houses, that made carpentry work difficult and frustrating. If you are subcontracting, be sure the people you employ have a savvy about old houses as well as competence and experience.

A wise house owner will continually and assiduously supervise all work, especially when it is occurring near something easily damaged. Anyone who trusts a laborer to work unattended risks a heartache. A house owner on the Near West Side who had engaged a plumber to install a new hot water heater on the second floor of his house left the plumber to his own designs for just half a day, and when he returned, he found huge slashes in his maple flooring where the plumber had cut space for new pipes. The only way to assure that work is done properly is to direct it in person. One building owner stood right up on the scaffolding with the bricklayer to guarantee that work was done the way he wanted it done.

Of course, directing or supervising tradesmen as they work presupposes some knowledge about the craft or repair. You can hardly protect yourself if you are totally ignorant of building renovation or repair. It is in your own interest to learn as much as possible about building rehabilitation before subcontracting. Not that you must become an expert in every building discipline. What you need is a sense of what the renovation entails, the dangers and difficulties of certain repairs, and the general order of events and costs. Even if you have engaged an architect, you should make an effort to learn and understand what is supposed to happen during the renovation to insure that it will happen.

Moreover, some contractors and tradesmen will gull a house owner into doing something he does not want done. Owners of houses with tile or slate roofs are likely to hear roofers say, "You can't repair that roof, but I can put up a new asphalt roof that will look just as good." A house owner who wants his parapet wall repaired by corbeling the bricks will be told by a mason, "You don't want corbeled brick, you want straight brick." Generally these flat statements mean that the tradesman does not have the ability to do the work you want done, but he would like to get paid for what he can do. And you must be prepared to insist that workmen rectify work done wrong. You must live with uncorrected mistakes, not the workmen, and crooked walls, windows out of square, and hot showers that capriciously turn cold can become incredibly irritating. You must be determined to get what you want and what you are paying for.

As with general contractors, all contracts with subcontractors should be detailed and comprehensive, specifying what the sub-contractor is to do, what materials will be used and how much he is to be paid. It is also wise to demand a waiver of lien from every subcontractor and building materials supplier. Even if a lien is without legal merit, it can cause considerable inconvenience. As building owner, you may have difficulty obtaining a bank loan, selling the building or closing out the Building Permit with the Building Department if a lien is on the building's title. One legal option worth considering is a deadline clause in the contract. Several house owners have found that subcontractors are casual about showing up for work, which is a problem if one subcontractor cannot begin work until another has finished. One house owner had his renovation delayed several months because the electrician failed to start work when promised, and without electrical service other subcontractors could not see or use power tools. A void or penalty clause in the contract might help eliminate subcontractor scheduling problems.

As with all contracts, unless you are knowledgeable in law, have a lawyer approve all contracts before you sign them. In addition, before subcontractors begin any work be sure they have insurance, both liability and workmen's compensation. Usually a standard home owner's insurance policy provides enough liability coverage for a building owner acting as his own general contractor. However, home owner's insurance usually requires the insured building be occupied. As many renovations are done with the building unoccupied, a special liability and fire insurance policy will be needed, which is usually more expensive. In such cases, you should talk to a reliable insurance broker even before buying the building.

BUILDING CODES AND PERMITS

Before any major work can begin, a Permit must be obtained from the City of Chicago — Department of Buildings. If a general contractor has been engaged to conduct the renovation, it is his responsibility to obtain all necessary permits and to assure that all repair work is done in conformity with the Building Codes. In Chicago, only certified plumbers and electricians are allowed to perform major work in their respective jurisdictions, and it is their responsibility to obtain a permit. If any work is going to be done to alter the structural composition of a house — moving, removing, replacing a post, pilaster, beam or enlarging an opening in an exterior wall, for examples — you will have to have an architect or structural engineer submit four sets of floor plans to obtain a Permit. The Building Department will allow a building owner to draw his own plans, and they offer some architectural consulting service (Room 804, City Hall), when an old house is being restored to its original floor layout, and if no load-bearing structures are altered.

If you are going to do work yourself or subcontract, then you must become familiar with Building Department procedures and the Building Codes or risk additional expenses or unnecessary delays. If materials are used that don't meet Code requirements, the Building Department usually demands they be removed. One renovator caused a long delay by not having a water resistant floor covering over the wood subflooring, as the Code requires, when his plumber came to install bathroom fixtures.

The Building Codes of Chicago can be obtained from only one place in Chicago — the publisher, Index Publishing Corporation. The complete Building Codes cost $18.85 by mail or $17.30 if purchased at Index's office. However, the bulk of the Building Code is not germane to residential renovation. Those sections pertinent to residents are in the Structural Section, $7.50 by mail or $6.30 at Index's office; the Electrical Code, $7.50 by mail or $6.30 at Index's office; and the Plumbing Code, $3.25 by mail or $2.10 at Index's office. (All prices are 1978.) Index Publishing is located at 323 West Randolph Street, 60606. Naturally, if purchasing by mail, provide a mailing address.

If only a few parts of the Code are needed, the Municipal Reference Library, open weekdays 8:30 to 5:00 on the 10th floor of City Hall, has copies and a copying machine. Likewise, the Central Library (in the temporary Mandel Building location) has a set of Building Codes on reserve in the Business and Industry Department.

In Chicago, a permit is required for all construction except "for minor repairs to maintain existing parts of a building." Therefore, a permit is not needed to strip woodwork, sand floors, fill plaster cracks, fix a leaking faucet, or cover a crack in the roofing. Anything not a minor repair will require a permit — new roofing, a new furnace, new siding, moving load-bearing members, new plumbing or electrical wiring, etc. All work, except plumbing and electrical, will be covered by one permit. As the phrase "for minor repairs to maintain" is somewhat vague, ask someone from the office of Permit Application Assistance, Room 800, City Hall or call 744-3175 or 744-3490 if there is a question whether a permit is needed.

An application for permit can be obtained at the permit application desk on the eighth floor of City Hall (121 N. LaSalle) in room 800. Usually there is a stack of applications and accompanying instruction sheets on the desk. If not, ask.

The Permit fee depends on the amount of work to be done. It is determined by the rate of $3 per $1,000 estimated renovation cost plus $20 for fire escape alterations (if needed), $6.50 for a new roof (if needed) and $12.50 for a warm air furnace installation (if needed). The minimum fee will be $20, the first $10 of which is paid at the beginning of permit processing.

Only after a permit has been obtained can work begin. The permit must be prominently displayed, such as on the inside of a first floor window or door. If work has not begun within six months, an extension for another six months from the Building Department at twenty-five percent charge of original fee will be needed. At critical stages in the renovation, for instance after plumbing, electrical and structural repairs have been made but before these repairs have been concealed by the installation of new walls or drywall, Building Inspectors are supposed to inspect the work for Code compliance. Then the Building Permit will be closed.

Chicago's Building Department has been the center of controversy in recent years. At times, the inspection of new work has been sporadic and cursory. At times, inspectors have been downright corrupt. The *Sun-Times* "Mirage" series and CBS's *Sixty Minutes* in early 1978 highlighted what many building owners have long known. Some years ago bribery solicitations became such a problem to renovators in the Old Town area that residents sought judicial relief. After several indictments were gained by the use of marked money, the practice subsided. Unfortunately, much of the corruption problem that plagues renovators is caused by other, more venal house owners who have discovered that they can save some money by bribing Building Inspectors to okay conditions that violate the Building Codes. It is these people who create an environment of corruption that makes life difficult for everyone else.

Based on the experience of others, the best defense for anyone solicited for a bribe by an Inspector is simply not to submit to intimidation. If the solicitation is in the form of a hint, ignore it. If the solicitation is overt, be clear and adamant that extortion will not be tolerated. If it appears that the inspector is going to go to the mat over this, which isn't likely, in Chicago use clout. Besides notifying a lawyer, try the local community organization. Community organizations often have good connections in Government and the media. A corrupt building inspctor is not likely to risk being the subject of attention in the press for a few dollars.

7

The Exterior Repair

The repair of any building must start with the exterior. It makes no sense to invest time and money on interior repair or redecoration when, because of exterior damage, that interior is exposed to destruction by weather.

But while a typical renovation begins with exterior REPAIR, the exterior APPEARANCE is usually left until last. With so many demands on finances at the outset of renovation, esthetic concerns must usually give way to practical necessities. Furthermore, for most people a clean, pleasant interior is a higher priority than an attractive exterior. In some cases, however, practical and esthetic concerns overlap. For example, masonry in need of tuckpointing should receive immediate attention to prevent water from entering and damaging the wall interior. However, the most convenient time to clean masonry — a purely esthetic exercise — is just prior to tuckpointing. Here again, careful planning is essential.

ROOFS

Exterior repair starts with the roof. The roof takes the brunt of nature's abuse, and a damaged roof causes more interior destruction than any other exterior defect. Unless the roof was recently recovered, you should expect to recover your roof not long after purchasing your old house.

Two kinds of roof prevail in old Chicago residential buildings: the flat roof, and the pitched roof, usually with a front-facing gable. Since such roofs cannot be seen from street level, they play little or no role in the esthetic design of the building, and modern materials can be used for their repair. Those rare roofs that do have an esthetic function, usually roofs of slate, clay tile or glazed tile, should of course be repaired rather than replaced with some other material (see chapter nine).

Flat roofs are commonly covered either by tar and gravel or by roll roofing. Tar and gravel is the older method, but it is still quite common. A tar and gravel roof consists of alternate layers of roofing paper and tar, topped by a layer of white gravel to protect the tar from the drying effect of direct sunlight. Roll roofing consists of a waterproof asphalt- or tar-impregnated felt, applied with a roofing cement to the roof boards or to an earlier layer of felt roll.

The pitched roofs on most late nineteenth and early twentieth century Chicago houses are covered with asphalt shingle or asphalt roll. On newer buildings asphalt shingles are predominant, but on older gable roofs, particularly in the inner city, asphalt roll is much more common. Asphalt roll is less expensive, easier to apply, and just as effective as shingle, but it is not as long lasting because it has less weight. Fifteen to twenty years is about as long as you can expect it to last. A good shingle roof should last five to ten years longer.

Re-roofing a pitched roof with new asphalt shingles or roll requires no elaborate tools or skills. Nevertheless, most owners of old houses opt for professional roofers because the money they might save is not worth the time and effort they will surely spend to do the job themselves. On a typical gable roof of 3,000 square feet, the cost for a ninety-pound asphalt roll roof installed by a contractor is about $900. For 240-pound self-sealing asphalt shingle, the cost will be approximately double that. A do-it-yourselfer could save about $400 using asphalt roll and twice that for self-sealing asphalt shingle, but against this saving must be weighed the amount of time that he would end up spending on his roof. A good roofing crew can easily cover a 3,000 square foot roof in one or two days. An amateur may take one to two weeks, and if the weather should turn nasty there is a risk that some of his efforts will be undone. If you plan to recover your roof during a summer vacation, you may end up scurrying to finish the job on weekends or late at night because your vacation was swallowed up by the typhoon season. One final factor you should consider before venturing up on your roof is your own personal safety. Most Chicago gable roofs are very steeply pitched. Saving a few hundred dollars is not worth a broken neck.

If you do decide to hazard re-roofing on your own, you will find that the work requires more physical exertion than manual skill. Probably the most difficult aspect of roofing with asphalt is attaching flashing properly to chimneys, flues, and walls. If any gaps are left between the flashing and a wall or chimney, water will flow and collect under the roof covering. The procedure for asphalt shingle or roll installation is described in virtually every home repair manual, and several shingle manufacturers and associations, such as the Asphalt Roofing Manufacturers Association, have published their own installation manuals for free distribution through supply outlets. These are as good as any "how-to" home repair book on sale in bookstores.

A pitched roof can generally be recovered by applying a new layer of asphalt shingle or roll over the old roof covering. However, if the roof has been left unattended and leaking for some time, roof boards may have begun to rot and the roof covering will have to be removed to replace them. With a pitched roof, signs of rot may be visible from the attic side of the roof. Since most old houses with pitched roofs already have several layers of roof covering, often including the original slate shingle, a large street gondola will probably have to be rented to cart away the several thousand pounds of discarded material.

Flat roofs can be recovered only by professional roofers, unless you happen to have a tar-melting pot available. However, many renovators do repair their flat roofs when damage is no more extensive than cracks in the felt roll. The repair procedure is described in most "how-to" home repair books, and it entails cutting out the damaged area, filling in the hole with new roofing felt, and sealing with trowelable roofing asphalt and liquid sealant. Of course, when a roof is in such a condition that cracks, blisters or loose flashing continually appear, it is time to think about a new roof. Still, it is possible to stretch the life of a flat roof for a few years.

As noted earlier, the traditional coverings on flat roofs are tar and gravel or impregnated felt roll. A new roofing system for flat roofs that offers some benefits under certain circumstances is exterior rigid roof insulation. This material, which consists of two-inch-thick panels of urethane or fiberglass, or a composite of urethane and fiberglass, laid over the roof deck and then covered with a layer of tar and gravel, was developed for use on commercial buildings. It is rarely installed on houses, since greater insulation can usually be obtained by insulating the attic. However, some old Chicago houses with flat roofs were built with no access to the attic crawl space. To insulate the attic in such a house requires tearing part or all of the ceiling down, which is expensive and, if the ceiling is ornate and attractive, undesirable. The other solution to this problem, pumping insulation into the attic through small holes in the ceiling or roof, has not proven to be very effective. Moreover this method, which lacks a vapor barrier, may allow moisture to condense under the roof and drip down, staining the ceiling below.

Rigid roof insulation for a 3,000 square foot flat roof will cost approximately $1,000 installed. The best brand is a matter of dispute, but the composite type seems to be preferable. There are a dozen or so manufacturers, including Johns-Manville (Fesco-Foam), Owens-

Corning (FURI), Grefco (Permalite) and Celotex (Tempchek). If you decide to install rigid roof insulation, you should seek bids from contractors who do commercial or industrial as well as residential roofing. The smaller roofing contractors usually have had little experience with these materials as so far there has been little demand from residential customers.

Roof gutters and downspouts must also be functional to prevent damage to the building's exterior. If water is allowed to run down exterior walls, it can leach out mortar in masonry, rot siding, cause unsightly and permanent stains, and permit foundation damage or water seepage into the basement. Repairing or replacing gutters and downspouts is another home repair within the ability of most house owners. Consult the "how-to" home repair manuals or the free booklets published by manufacturers for detailed instructions. The most common mistakes made by do-it-yourselfers: installing gutters without proper downward slope (leaving water to stand in the gutter or flow over), not sealing gutter or downspout joints properly (allowing water to leak) and using steel nails to install aluminum gutters. Steel nails should never be used with aluminum as electrolysis between the two metals will cause the aluminum to deteriorate rapidly. Gutters can be purchased at building supply outlets and generally cost about seventy cents per foot for seamless aluminum.

EXTERIOR WALLS

The exterior walls of a building should be nearly as impervious to weather as the roof. Wind and rain most frequently enter exterior walls around window and door frames. Frames are sealed with caulk, which will dry out, crack and fall away from the frames with time. If there is anything a building owner certainly can do in the way of self-repair, it is recaulking the door and window frames. Butyl caulk can be obtained at any hardware store and can be applied with an in-

A badly damaged wood facade can be "repaired" by applying false siding on top of the original clapboard.

expensive caulking gun or putty knife. In addition to sealing out rain, caulk prevents a significant heat loss during winter.

On old houses of wood construction, problems often arise with window sills. Window sills should be angled slightly down and away from the window so water cannot flow back into the building. A rotted or cracked sill may allow water to enter the exterior wall and cause severe damage. Replacing a rotted or damaged window sill is another task you as house owner can accomplish yourself. The procedure is described in most repair books, the necessary tools are nothing more than a hammer, chisel and crowbar, and replacement sills, milled with a beveled angle, are a stock lumberyard item.

Because wood is more perishable than stone or brick, it is often supposed that old wood-clad houses will have more serious problems with exterior deterioration than masonry houses. This is not necessarily the case. A wood-clad exterior will of course degenerate if it is neglected, but most wood-clad houses in Chicago were long ago covered with false siding of one kind or another — asphalt, asbestos, masonite, permastone, aluminum or vinyl. While the application of false siding generally spoils a building's proportions and appearance, it does protect walls from serious deterioration. Masonry exteriors, on the other hand, are by no means "maintenance-free." Water and ice attack the mortar in the joints, which finally cracks and breaks away. As the mortar disintegrates, water is allowed to enter the wall, eventually causing serious structural deterioration. To prevent this, masonry must be retuckpointed periodically, an unavoidable repair.

The disintegration of masonry may not be limited only to the mortar. Sometimes the brick itself is in bad condition, particularly if the building has been cleaned by sandblasting. Sandblasting is the most common method for cleaning masonry — so much so that the words *clean* and *sandblast* are often used interchangeably. But sandblasting can be very damaging. When brick is fired, it forms a skin much as a loaf of bread forms an outer crust when it is baked. This "skin" is impervious to exterior water but will allow interior water

It is far preferable, esthetically speaking, actually to repair and repaint the original wood siding and ornamentation.

to pass through. If it is destroyed or damaged, the brick will become porous and water will penetrate the surface, freeze and expand, causing the brick to flake or chip away — a process called *spalling*. In addition to spalling, moisture that enters the brick interior often causes salts to dissolve and recrystallize on the brick's surface, forming an unattractive white film. This process is called *efflorescence*. Most experts recommend that brick never be sandblasted.

The standard technique for protecting sandblasted masonry is to seal the brick from moisture by spray-applying a chemical sealant, usually silicone, although paraffin and acrylic sealants are sometimes used. Silicone sealants are preferred over acrylics because they are nearly invisible, while acrylic sealants often leave a visible sheen. However, silicone sealants last only four to seven years, and then they must be reapplied to prevent renewed spalling and efflorescence. Because masonry sealants are impermanent, owners of buildings with sandblasted masonry will always have to watch vigilantly for incipient deterioration.

How masonry should be cleaned is determined mainly by whether it has already been sandblasted. Once the brick surface has been destroyed, there is no compelling reason not to sandblast again. If, however, the brick surface is original and unscathed, the least damaging professional method of removing accumulated grime is steam cleaning, perhaps with a mild detergent if necessary. Some professionals use muriatic acid (a mild solution of hydrochloric acid) for cleaning. Muriatic acid can be effective, but it must be used with caution. The acid must not be left on too long, and a neutralizer should be washed over the masonry afterward to prevent chemical burns.

To remove paint from face brick, the least damaging method is to use proprietary chemical strippers that dissolve the paint film so that it can be flushed off by a stream of water. In the case of sandblasted masonry, paint has probably been absorbed into the brick, and additional sandblasting may be the only effective way of removing the paint.

Paint on undamaged face brick usually will peel off, while paint on damaged face brick or common brick soaks in. Notice that the mortar joints on this facade were painted a contrasting color, something rarely done in America but common in Europe.

Tuckpointing and cleaning masonry is a strenuous and dirty job, which is why most building owners contract professionals rather than doing the work themselves. Yet despite the unpleasantness, it does not require expensive tools or delicate skills and is therefore a project most house owners can successfully accomplish. If you must do some renovation work due to financial limitations, it is wiser to attempt retuckpointing and cleaning your masonry than to take on less tedious but riskier projects such as electrical rewiring or plumbing repair.

To clean and retuckpoint masonry, you will have to rent or borrow scaffolding. It is simply too arduous and dangerous to work on the top of a straight ladder. Work on a masonry wall proceeds from the top down — otherwise flushed dirt and dropped mortar spoil the clean area below. However, before spending money on scaffolding, it is usually wise to test your technique on a small inconspicuous area of the lower facade.

Besides the scaffolding you will need trowels, striking tools, chisels and something to mix the mortar in. Mortar can be purchased from building supply outlets as a pre-mix that just requires water, or it can be prepared in the traditional manner by mixing masonry cement, lime putty, sand and water. Tuckpointing is described in most home repair books. It is basically a simple procedure — a chisel or old screwdriver is used to loosen old mortar, the loose mortar is flushed out of the mortar joints with water from a garden hose, mortar is forced into the joints with a trowel while the masonry is still wet (to provide a better bond) and then a striking tool is used to shape the mortar in the joint. About the only mistake you can make is to tuckpoint in direct sunlight, which causes the mortar to dry too quickly, weakening its bond to the brick.

The best do-it-yourself method for cleaning masonry is to scrub the bricks by hand, using a strong detergent and a soft nylon brush. A wire brush should never be used on face brick, as it will cause surface damage. Muriatic acid, which is available at any building sup-

Sandstone and limestone can be more fragile than brick or wood.
First the stone becomes unsightly; then, if spalling is not arrested,
more serious structural problems develop.

ply outlet and most hardware and paint stores, can be used to remove efflorescence and encrusted dirt. If you use muriatic acid, be sure to wear splash goggles and rubber gloves and have running water available.

To remove paint from face brick, the best approach is to use chemical strippers. Most large paint outlets sell paint stripper for exterior masonry at about $10 per gallon. How much stripper will be required depends upon how thick the paint film is. Usually one application of exterior paint stripper will dissolve only two layers of paint. If the paint is thick, the stripper may have to be flushed and reapplied several times. Again, it is usually a good idea to test the stripper on a small area of the facade before making a big investment in a particular brand. If the stripper fails to remove the paint completely, it is probably because the wall has been sandblasted, and it will have to be sandblasted again by a professional.

Stone facades, like masonry and wood, will deteriorate if neglected. Throughout the city there are old greystones and brownstones with large areas of deteriorating surface. On some buildings deterioration has reached the point where huge hunks of stone have sloughed off. Sandstone and many types of limestone are extremely vulnerable to degeneration. They are porous by nature, so moisture can penetrate and cause the stone to crack and spall. Besides their natural vulnerability, sandstone and especially limestone have suffered from Chicago's air pollution. For most of the lifetime of these houses, air here has been heavily polluted with sulfur dioxide from the burning of high-sulfur coal. Sulfur dioxide in the presence of air-borne moisture forms sulfuric acid, which is as pernicious to limestone as it is to the lung tissue of humans. Thus, through the action of air pollution and weather, many limestone facades are in bad condition.

If you own a building with a severely deteriorated facade of sandstone or limestone, you have a problem for which there is no adequate solution. The standard repair technique for spalled and deteriorated sections of sandstone is to fill in the areas of decomposed stone with a mortar of matching color. However, it is difficult to match the colors of stone. Skilled stone masons, of which there are few in Chicago, will often try to match stone colors by grinding off particles from an inconspicuous area of the facade to mix with the mortar. But even this often fails, as evidenced by the many woe-gone brownstones around Chicago. Repair of corroded limestone is generally more successful than that of brown sandstone. The usual repair technique involves covering the limestone completely with a stucco-like mortar that includes silicone to resist renewed spalling. The mortar has a color and texture similar to that of the original limestone, and therefore need not spoil the facade's appearance. However, contractors usually apply the stucco mortar over the mortar joints as well as the stones, which detracts from the facade's original appearance. If a contractor cannot be hectored into leaving the mortar joints uncovered, they can be painted. This is commonly done in Europe.

Cleaning a stone facade is generally beyond the ability of most house owners. Because limestone and sandstone are porous, paint will usually penetrate the stone surface and sandblasting will be about the only effective way of removing paint or deeply embedded dirt. Sandblasted limestone or sandstone facades, like brick, must be sealed with silicone, and you will always have to remain alert for signs of spalling. For a limestone facade suffering only from surface dirt or stains, many professionals prefer to steam clean, with a mild lye or abrasive if necessary.

WINDOWS

After many years of use and abuse, it is unlikely that windows in an unrenovated old house will not need some attention. Home repair manuals describe procedures for repairing damaged window sash.

Certainly some of the easier repairs, such as replacing deteriorated putty, fixing loose sash, repairing sash springs or counterweights, or tightening sash frames, can be handled adequately by most house owners. However, removing sash from jambs in many old houses is more difficult than the typical home repair manual suggests, and if you are not an experienced wood worker, this is best left to professionals. Glass retail outlets and glazing contractors located in old neighborhoods often specialize in window repair and maintenance. If a window sash has completely deteriorated from rot, it will have to be replaced, and if it is an odd size, as windows in old houses often are, the sash will have to be custom-made at a millwork. There are several small millworks around Chicago that will fabricate new sash. The millwork that seem to have garnered the most business for new sash is Hohmeier, at 2011 W. Belmont in Chicago.

Stained glass windows of course present special problems, for they are fragile and expensive to repair. They also seem to attract rocks. It may be prudent to install a protective storm window of plastic over your stained glass. Plastic is preferable to plate glass because it is more resistant to impact, though it does have drawbacks — the surface is susceptible to scratching and over time a haze may develop. The most commonly used plastics for windows are plexiglas and lexan. Lexan, though more expensive, is the best for window panes. A six square foot storm window of lexan (a typical size for stained glass) costs about $60, $50 for the lexan and $10 for an aluminum frame with baked enamel coating in brown.

8

The Interior Renovation

STRUCTURAL REPAIR

The interior renovation must begin with the repair of any damaged or weakened structural elements. Because most Victorian houses were well constructed, and because they are not really all that old, most in the Chicago area are still structurally sound. Most old houses will have walls out of square or floors not level, but usually this is due to past settling, not to structural damage. In larger old houses, it is likely that the renovation will start with the removal of plasterboard walls that converted the house from a family residence to a boardinghouse.

If an old house does have structural problems, chances are they lie in the flooring. In some of the oldest Chicago neighborhoods, it was common to build three-flat and some four-flat buildings with a below-grade first floor rather than with a complete basement. Because the first floor flooring is in such close proximity to moist earth, floor joists of the below-grade floor often rot. A sound repair requires taking up the flooring and sub-flooring — a major project that usually costs several thousand dollars. A few building owners have tried to save money by pumping concrete under the floor instead of replacing the rotted joists. This is a structurally viable technique, but it has rarely provided any savings.

Wood as it ages will dry and shrink, and this too can cause structural problems with floors in old houses. As floor joists shrink, a space may open up between joist and subflooring, causing the floor to creak and bounce. The solution is basically simple — wood shims are driven into the gap between joists and subflooring, and bridging, which was not often used by Victorian builders, can be constructed between adjacent joists to distribute weight evenly. If the damaged joist is a first floor support, there is little problem — the joist can be repaired from the basement. However, repairing a joist on an upper floor with a valuable and ornate plaster ceiling below can be a nightmare. To save the ceiling, renovation experts usually try to repair the joist by going through the floor above rather than the ceiling below. Sometimes experts attempt to remove the entire plaster ceiling intact, reinstalling it after repairing or replacing the damaged joist. Both methods are risky and expensive and require the direction of someone highly competent in old house restoration.

In some old houses, rot or shrinkage of floor joists may actually cause the ends of some of the joists to move off the foundation. If more than a few adjacent joists should pull free, a large section of the building will be hanging over the basement essentially without support. If this is left unattended for too long, the house will eventually collapse. Providing support for the free-hanging joists is relatively simple, but to do it without damage to the building interior is not. For structural support, a new girder is placed under and perpendicular to the unsupported floor joists. The girder is supported by posts with adjustable jacks that can be extended, raising the floor to its original level. However, the process of raising a floor causes a massive redistribution of weight throughout the building. If movement is too rapid, it can cause extensive damage to plaster walls and ceilings. (Of course, if the interior is going to be rebuilt anyway, this does not matter.) To avoid damage, restoration experts raise the floor very slowly, often taking several years to complete the process. This is not a job for amateurs.

More often than not, if an old house has structural damage, it has been caused by a previous owner rather than by natural aging. For instance, installing new plumbing lines in an old house is difficult because interior wall space or floor-ceiling space is usually insufficient to accommodate a large pipe. To make a pipe fit, sections of joists or studs must be cut away, or "notched," greatly reducing their structural strength. This work can be safely done by someone who knows what he is doing, but amateur plumbers almost always just saw away with no thought for the consequences, and even professional remodelers are notoriously cavalier about this problem because they know that the damage will not show up until long after they have been paid. One old house owner with a bathtub which vibrated when he took a bath discovered that the only thing preventing him from crashing to a watery death was a narrow section of notched joist. Moreover, wherever there is water there may be rot, and this rot is likely to occur in the notched sections of studs and joists. Springy floors in bathrooms and kitchens must be investigated, and certainly no remodeling of these rooms should go forward until any damage to joists and studs has been corrected.

ELECTRICAL SYSTEM

It is often said that Chicago is a good union town. For proof, there is the Building Code. In Chicago, a house owner is not permitted to do any electrical repair other than changing a light bulb or fuse, thereby insuring more work for the union electrician. Not that many people do not do much of their own electrical work anyway; they do. Some rewiring projects are not difficult, such as adding or moving an outlet when a house already has adequate electrical service, and there are dozens of "how-to" home repair books offering direction for the willing. Nevertheless, besides being illegal, an amateur rewiring job can prove dangerous. There have been several recent fires in Chicago, some with fatalities, attributed to the owner's improper rewiring. At the very least, no one should try to save money on electrical work by using materials of less than Code standards or by doing work he does not completely understand. The consequences are simply too costly.

Although it may be a certified electrician who installs the new service lines in an old house, it should be the owner who is concerned about where the lines are installed. It is easy to mark a symbol for a light switch on a floor plan blueprint. But the blueprint may not reveal the ornamental plasterwork that the electrician must cut through to place the switch where the floor plan shows it. An electrician installing new conduit will choose the easiest possible route. The owner, however, should look for a conduit route that minimizes damage to saveable walls and ceilings, because any increase in the cost of the rewiring job will be more than offset by later savings. Here again you have to coordinate your various projects, and you must stick to your guns when dealing with contractors and tradesmen.

In most wood-frame houses there should be little problem with interior damage from electrical rewiring since there is usually sufficient space between wall studs to run new conduit. The greatest frustrations arising from electrical rewiring occur in masonry buildings. Following the fires of 1871 and 1874, Chicagoans understandably became very fire conscious. Wood buildings were prohibited entirely within city limits and masonry houses were built to stringent new Building Codes. One requirement was for horizontal fire stops inside walls to prevent fire from spreading quickly through an entire building. These stops (there may be as many as five fire stops of wood or tile obstructing the space inside a masonry wall) make it virtually impossible to run conduit up through the wall without breaking the plaster. Opening and repairing interior walls with horizontal fire stops can actually cost more than the electrical work itself.

Fortunately, many old houses contain hidden areas that might provide an unobstructed space for running conduit. For example, you might find that a dumbwaiter shaft provides a convenient space to run conduit from cellar to the third floor. Non-functional chimneys can sometimes provide conduit runs, or there may be a usable space next to a chimney. However, you should never use that space if the chimney is functional, as this is both hazardous and illegal. Sometimes conduit can be run behind baseboards and wood trim. The baseboard is removed, studs are notched to accommodate the conduit, then the baseboard is reinstalled. If the baseboard is an expensive hardwood such as mahogany or oak and it begins to crack during removal, this approach should be abandoned. But if the baseboard is a common pine moulding replaceable from any lumberyard, then it does not matter if it cracks or shatters because new moulding will cost less than new plaster.

Finally, if an old house is in such disrepair that it must be totally rewired, probably walls will have to be opened for other repairs as well. If the plumbing is faulty, the plaster needs a lot of attention anyway, or if the house floor plan is being redesigned, the electrician should be able to do his job unobtrusively — so long as you plan ahead.

PLUMBING

In many old house renovations, plumbing repairs are the largest single expense. Furthermore, plumbing costs seem to be inflating faster than any other cost in the renovating field. For this reason it may not be wise to postpone plumbing repair.

The general condition of the plumbing can sometimes be determined by examining pipes in the cellar. Lead pipes are illegal in Chicago and should be replaced. In some houses a previous owner may have repaired plumbing with pipes of dissimilar metal. Dissimilar metal pipes usually corrode at the joint, and they should also be replaced. In many old houses the pipes are of galvanized iron, which normally lasts only twenty to thirty years. If the plumbing is old, you should not expect it to last much longer, and you should consider a new plumbing system.

In some cases the only way to determine the condition of the plumbing is to tear open a wall and examine the pipes. If the walls are in poor condition anyway, this makes little difference, but if they are in good condition, breaking into them can be cause for much anguish. Even so, if there is the slightest hint that the plumbing will not last much longer, it is best to have new plumbing installed.

Like electrical repair, plumbing repair in Chicago can be done legally only by a certified workman. Some mechanically-inclined house owners install their own bathroom or kitchen fixtures, but few attempt to install a complete new plumbing system. If anyone bewails the Plumbing Code of Chicago, it is not because do-it-yourself repair is prohibited but because plastic pipe cannot legally be used. Plumbing repair costs are often large, and plastic pipe could reduce those costs as it is cheaper than metal. However, the City of Chicago has banned all plastic pipe for safety reasons. While some plastic pipe will release cyanide gas when ignited, not all kinds will. Plastic pipe is allowed in most suburbs, and no known tragedies have resulted. Chicago renovators are being penalized by a needlessly large margin of safety. For those for whom cost is not limiting, copper pipes, the most expensive, are without question the best. They are long-lasting and corrosion resistant.

Although you as owner cannot do your own plumbing, you can control costs by considering where the plumbing fixtures should be placed. Moving a bathroom or kitchen can be very expensive, depending upon where they are moved. Plumbing in residential buildings is "stacked." The input pipes (risers) and the output pipe (waste stack) often serve more than a single bathroom or kitchen. Bathrooms directly above one another share the same risers and waste stack, as do bathrooms on opposite sides of a wall on the same floor. If a bathroom or kitchen is moved or an additional one constructed more than a few feet from the existing plumbing lines, new risers and a waste stack will have to be provided. This can be a major project, entailing opening up walls to install pipes, breaking apart the basement floor to connect the new waste stack, and opening the roof for the stack vent. Obviously, constructing new bathrooms or kitchens away from existing plumbing is going to be expensive. The time to be aware of plumbing expenses from new or moved fixtures is when the floor plans and building specifications are being drawn up. A responsible architect will point out to a client that moving or constructing a bathroom or kitchen in some parts of a house may be far more expensive than in other parts. If you are directing your own house renovation, you should find the least expensive locations for new bathrooms or kitchens before inviting plumbers to bid.

Victorian bathroom fixtures — clawfoot tubs, marble vanity tops, pedestal sinks — have been one of the last features of an old house to be appreciated again. As more and more people come to believe that an original bathroom is proper in an old house, removing original bathroom fixtures is increasingly likely to reduce a building's value. Unfortunately, many old tubs and sinks of porcelain enamel are badly stained, cracked or chipped. There really is no satisfactory solution to this problem. Dozens of companies are in the business of "porcelain refinishing" (usually listed in the Yellow Pages under Porcelain Enamel Repairing and Refinishing). Despite their claims to the contrary, however, they do not actually restore the enamel surface but rather cover it with an epoxy paint. Certainly the epoxy coat looks better than discolored or eroded porcelain, but it is usually guaranteed for no more than a year. You never know what it will eventually look like, and besides, to purists the epoxy and porcelain enamel just do not look the same. Old bathroom fixtures can sometimes be found in the salvage yard of a demolition company (for example, *Cleveland Wrecking,* on North Milwaukee in Chicago) or bathroom remodelers sometimes resale plumbing fixtures (for example *Sam Serota* on North Milwaukee, Chicago).

Restoring and repairing metal faucets is usually more successful. Pitted or stained faucets can be inexpensively replated, in either brass or chrome, by a metal refinisher such as *Art Metal Finishers,* at 6741

N. Clark, Chicago, *Junk Man Antiques* at 2154 N. Halsted, Chicago or *Custom Metal Polishing & Plating* at 1750 N. Campbell, Chicago. One warning about removing old faucets — because old plumbing is often fragile, some people have found that the simple repair or removal of a faucet leads to major plumbing work.

HEATING

There are essentially three different types of heating systems to be found in old Chicago houses: warm air, hot water and steam. Each of these systems may be fueled either by gas or by oil. The debate as to which of them is best is academic for most buyers because, short of completely rebuilding the interior of the house, the basic system with which the house was built will have to be retained.

Most smaller houses have warm air heat. If you find in your basement an enormous dome-shaped furnace with round ducts coming out of the top, what you have is the original gravity warm air unit. These systems rely on the fact that warm air naturally rises and cool air sinks. The registers will be flat on the floor in the various heated rooms, usually next to inside walls, and there will be several larger cold air return registers, usually next to outside walls, through which cold air is returned to the furnace to be heated again. Often these gravity systems were modernized by the addition of a blower to the original furnace, and by the installation of a new burner in the old furnace box. The point of the blower is to force the heated air through the ducts, thereby providing more even heat. In more thorough updating jobs, new ducts and registers were added onto the original system. These new registers were usually wall-mounted (since it makes more sense to blow warmed air across the room rather than at the ceiling) and where possible they were installed in outside walls, which became possible because the blower could force the warm air a greater distance from the furnace.

If you have one of the old gravity furnaces, even if it has been updated with a blower, at some point you will want to install a new furnace. A new forced-air furnace will be much more efficient, and it will be amazingly smaller than the old unit, perhaps even allowing you to convert the furnace room into space useful for some other purpose. If additional ducts have not been added to the original system, it is likely that new ducts will have to be installed to bring the system up to modern standards of comfort. Obviously this work should be completed before much interior restoration is done. If you do need a new furnace, it is a good idea to do a little independent research to find out what capacity you need. Too much capacity will result in inefficient operation, and your contractor may be tempted to sell you more furnace than you need.

Original hot water heating systems operate in principle very similarly to the old gravity warm-air systems. Hot water, being lighter than cold water, will rise through a system of pipes and radiators and, once cooled, will sink back to the boiler to be heated again. Just as the old warm-air systems were improved by the addition of a blower, hot water systems were often greatly improved by adding an electric pump to circulate the water. If your hot water system lacks a pump, you will want to install a new hydronic system, which can be hooked up to the existing supply pipes and radiators if they are in good shape.

However, if the existing pipes are not in good shape, you will have a difficult decision to make. The consequences of water leaks can be very serious, and the replacement of pipes, other than those easily accesible in the basement, will involve breaking into walls. As with any plumbing in an old house, it is better to be safe than sorry. Dubious parts of the system should be replaced before the interior work is started. Expert advice from a heating specialist will pay off in the long run.

Once the system is in good order, there are several maintenance jobs that you can do yourself. The radiators will occasionally need to be bled to remove trapped air, and shut-off valves on the radiator may need to be repacked if they leak. Consult any good home repair manual. In addition, many mechanically-inclined home owners with hot water systems make a point of keeping handy a large pipe wrench and an assortment of pipe plugs; it is sometimes possible to isolate a leaking part of the system, thereby enabling you to maintain some heat until a proper repair can be made. It must be said, however, that hot water systems are very difficult for the novice to work on. The pipes are large and the joints very difficult to budge without the right heavy-weight tools and a lot of physical strength.

A very common irritation with hot water systems is the problem of regulating the level of the heat in individual rooms. To some extent the shut-off valve on each radiator will allow you to control the temperature of that radiator, but closing the valve half-way will not give you half the heat. In fact, the slightest opening of the valve may give you more heat than you want, and it is highly unlikely that a single setting will be right for a range of outside temperatures. Generally it is best to leave these valves either fully open or completely closed, and to solve the problem of an overheated room by installing a smaller radiator or a radiator cover. But if you find that a room is comfortable with the radiator shut off (as might well be the case if you have installed storm windows or upgraded the insulation) be sure that the supply line is not in an outside wall. Closing the valve may allow water to be trapped in the line, and on a really cold day the water may freeze and burst the pipe.

Steam systems are very simple in theory. Water is made into steam in a boiler, and the steam rises under pressure through supply pipes to the radiators, condenses there, losing most of its heat, and returns in the form of water down the same pipe (or sometimes down a separate return line) to the boiler to be heated again. In practice, however, these systems can be tricky, and dangerous for a do-it-yourselfer to work with. High temperatures and pressures are involved, and misguided tinkering with the boiler could cause an explosion.

Still, steam heat is perfectly safe if the equipment is properly maintained. If your old house has a gas burner, the best first step is to call the gas company to have the boiler checked. The gas company service man will have a look at the entire boiler as well as the gas burner, and he can be trusted to give you a knowledgeable appraisal of the system in general. Unfortunately, boiler repair companies cannot always be trusted to give you good advice; they would like to sell you a new boiler. A typical con job goes like this: you receive a card in the mail which offers a furnace inspection for $5.00. The service man arrives, looks over your boiler, and tells you that there is a leak which he can probably fix by injecting silica, for a $70 charge. This measure fails to correct the problem, but since he is such a fine fellow he offers to apply the $70 charge against the price of a new boiler. The fact is that steam boilers often have a long life, and even if your equipment looks to you as if it was made shortly after the Civil War, it may be sound or at least repairable. If you do need a new boiler, the cost will be high, certainly over $3,000 for a unit capable of heating a large house or a three-flat.

There are a number of minor maintenance jobs on a steam system that can be safely taken on by a non-professional. The relief valves on the radiators deteriorate quickly, but they are readily available and simple to replace. The water level in the boiler needs to be checked frequently. If the level is manually controlled, you will have to remember to add water frequently during the heating season. If the boiler has an automatic feed, this unit will need to be drained about once a month in the winter. The efficiency of the system can be improved by insulating the mains and risers in the basement. Safe procedures for all these jobs can be found in home repair manuals with sections on heating.

Perhaps the most frequent complaint about steam heat is noisy radiators. A certain amount of noise seems to be inevitable, but much of it is caused by water trapped in the bottom of radiators. When a building settles, the radiators often become tilted away from their supply pipes, preventing the flow of water out of the radiator. When this happens the steam has to force its way up through the trapped water, which reduces the efficiency of the radiator and produces the familiar clunking and gurgling. The easy solution is to boost up the low end of the radiator with wooden blocks so that the radiator inclines slightly (use a spirit level) toward the supply pipe. Leaky radiator shut-off valves are a frequent problem with steam systems as well as with hot water heat. Often the solution is to repack the valve stem, a fairly simple repair.

Even if you leave the maintenance of the system to a professional, you should acquaint every member of your household with the fact that the radiator shut-off valves must always be either fully open (but not jammed open) or fully closed. These valves are not intended to provide a means of regulating the level of heat in the radiator, other than shutting it off altogether. A partially-open valve will cause water to be trapped in the bottom of the radiator, and this will produce the problems mentioned above.

All modern heating systems are controlled by a thermostat which switches the furnace on or off in response to the temperature of the room where the thermostat is located. The furnace will be entirely ignorant of the temperature of other rooms, and thermostats can be easily "fooled" by drafts from windows or doors or by the heat from fireplaces. Before you conclude that you have a faulty thermostat or furnace and call the repairman, consult a manual that explains how your system is supposed to function. (Blowers and circulation pumps, for instance, do not switch on until the temperature in the furnace or boiler reaches a pre-set temperature.) If your thermostat is faulty, you should consider replacing it with a clock thermostat which will automatically lower the temperature six or seven degrees at night to save energy. In many cases these clock thermostats simply replace the old unit and do not require any new wiring.

If you do intend virtually to rebuild the interior of your house, you will have the opportunity to choose between various types of heating systems. Given this choice, most select forced air heat because of its relative simplicity and the ease with which heat can be regulated in each room by means of dampers in the ducts and registers. But if the old steam or hot water system is beyond repair, and yet much of the original house interior is worth preserving, new hydronic hot water heat may be the best choice. The trouble with warm air heat is that the ducts must be quite large. Hot water supply pipes are much smaller, and they can be installed with much less damage to existing walls. Modern hydronic systems often use baseboard radiators, which provide more even heat and are less obtrusive than the old freestanding radiators. A solution that leads to even less damage to the interior is electric heat, which is by far the easiest and cheapest system to install. Additional advantages of electric heat are that it is very clean, virtually maintenance-free and can be regulated on a room-by-room basis. The disadvantage, however, is the very high operating cost. They are reasonably competitive with oil- or gas-fueled systems only if the house is extraordinarily well insulated, and it is very difficult and certainly very expensive to bring an old house up to the necessary level of heat tightness.

In some cases, especially in larger houses, the solution is to install several separate systems or even a combination of different systems. If the original equipment works well except for a room or two, some supplementary electric heat may well be the least expensive solution. If finding room for warm air ducts is a problem, several small furnaces serving separate areas of the house might make sense. Modern forced-air furnaces are so small that they can be tucked away in closets or other small areas, with ducts running through the walls to nearby rooms. Some renovators have even installed a furnace in the attic. In three-flats with outmoded steam heat, a good solution may be to install separate forced-air furnaces on each floor, stacked one above the other so they can be served by a common flue.

AIR CONDITIONING

Houses with forced-air heat are the easiest to aircondition because useable duct work is already in place. A cooling unit can be added when a new furnace is installed. It must be pointed out, however, that few old house owners who have added central airconditioning in this way have been entirely satisfied. Warm air systems are after all designed to take advantage of the fact that warm air rises. The registers are placed low on the walls or in the floor, and the registers above the first floor are made smaller because an open staircase functions as a huge duct to carry warm air upstairs. The problem of cooling a house is in many ways the exact reverse. The registers should ideally be high on the walls, and the upper floors of the house, which require less heat, will require more air conditioning. For these reasons central airconditioning in an old house all too often results in either a comfortable ground floor and a hot upstairs, or else a comfortable upstairs (if the air conditioner has sufficient capacity) and a ground floor the temperature of a meat locker.

Since well-built old houses will generally stay fairly comfortable on the ground floor even in hot weather, a good solution, and by far the least expensive, is to install a bedroom window unit where necessary, and a good attic fan to cool down the rest of the house at night. Another solution is to install a cooling unit in the attic, which makes the installation of ducts to rooms below quite easy.

Central airconditioning a house with steam or hot water heat is an expensive proposition because air ducts will have to be installed, but it can be done. If you decide to go this route, be sure to locate a contractor who has done a lot of work on old houses.

FIREPLACES

For nineteenth century Chicagoans fireplaces were a necessity. To present-day old house owners they are in danger of becoming an obsession. The sale of an old house now sometimes hinges upon an expert's evaluation of the chimney's condition: if the fireplace cannot be made to work, the buyer looks elsewhere.

The most common repair done on old fireplace chimneys is chimney relining. Over time, mortar in chimney masonry joints will deteriorate and fall out, just as mortar in exterior masonry deteriorates. If the mortar degradation is severe enough, there is a possibility that holes have opened, creating a potential hazard. Exhaust gases could enter the house by escaping through a chimney hole, asphixiating the inhabitants, or a hot cinder could escape and start a fire in the wood framing around the chimney. To prevent such a disaster, a metal flue liner can be installed in the chimney from the top. The cost for galvanized iron chimney lining is approximately $14 per foot.

However, despite the potential hazards, whether or not a chimney needs to be relined is a matter of contention among experts. Certainly fires and suffocation have been traced to deteriorated chimneys. However, for gas or a cinder to escape through a hole in the chimney, the chimney must be blocked somewhere so that it does not draw properly. If a chimney is drawing air properly, there is a negative pressure inside the chimney and gas or cinders would have to travel against a strong air current to escape through a hole or crack. For this reason some experts argue that finding and clearing any blockage will make the chimney safe. This disagreement applies, however, only to FIREPLACE chimneys and flues. A chimney serving a FURNACE should have a stainless steel flue liner. One old house owner vented a furnace through an unlined chimney and the heat alone caused plaster to crack and fall off walls near the chimney.

If your fireplace fails to draw properly, the cause is probably a blocked flue. Animals of various kinds are fond of building nests in chimneys, and the solution may involve nothing more than removing leaves, sticks and so on from the flue. An inexpensive screen over the top of the flue will prevent animal incursions. Since flues should be cleaned periodically of soot (an inexpensive maintenance operation costing approximately $80) when a chimney is cleaned by a contractor, an animal screen should be installed also.

However, many fireplaces draft poorly or not at all because of a collapsed flue. In multi-story buildings a chimney may have a number of flues serving various fireplaces. It is quite common for the brick partitions between flues to collapse, blocking the draft. The only way to fix this problem is to open the chimney and rebuild the flues, which can be quite expensive, especially if interior walls have to be opened to get at the chimney.

In recent years many owners of old houses have complained that their fireplaces will not draw even though the flue is clear and the firebox properly designed. The cause of this mysterious dysfunction lies in the energy crisis. With the rising cost of fuel for heating, building owners have installed storm windows, caulked window and door frames and put in weather-stripping. These measures against heat loss have been very effective, so effective that the house becomes essentially airtight, and air movement in the chimney stops. The remedy is simple — open a window slightly when the fireplace is in use.

A fireplace is not a very efficient source of heat. Often it will pull more heat out of a room through the chimney than it radiates into the room from fire in the firebox, and of course if you have to open a window to make the fire draw, your problem is even worse. If you want to use your fireplace as an ancillary furnace and not just for pleasure, the best approach is to have a professional chimney contractor build a duct with damper from the firebox to an outside source of air. With such a duct, the fireplace will not draw warm air from the interior of the house. This is a relatively simple and inexpensive operation if the chimney is on an exterior wall. For chimneys in the building interior, it is usually prohibitively expensive.

Following the Victorian era, wood-burning fireplaces were no longer in vogue, and it was not uncommon for mantels to be torn out and fireplaces bricked up. There is still a lively commerce in new and original fireplace mantels in the Chicago area for anyone who needs to replace a missing or damaged mantel. Many antique stores in the area carry wood fireplace mantels, although often the mantels did not originate here and are not Victorian in style. *Just Everything* at 2965 N. Lincoln Avenue in Chicago usually has a large stock of common wood mantels. *Hawk and Handsaw* at 2029 N. Clybourn, *Antiques 'N' Things* at 1323 W. Webster and the *Renovation Source* at 3514 N. Southport also usually have a selection of salvaged wood mantels. *King Chimney & Fireplace Company* in Chicago. a local repair contractor, has a large selection of Victorian wood mantels salvaged from old Chicago area houses, as does *Newberry's* at 1524 S. Peoria, Chicago. Some paint strippers, such as *Sunset Strippers* at 3433 N. Halsted, Chicago, also have salvaged fireplace mantels on sale. *The Roman Marble Company* at 120 W. Kinzie in Chicago has a stock of Victorian marble mantels salvaged from old houses and new marble mantels imported from Italy.

If you have a marble mantel, you must be extremely careful of the marble's fragility. Some chimney repair contractors will not work on a fireplace with a marble mantel, as the owner will blame them if the marble is broken even though it is difficult to avoid damage. Some marble is so weak that if it is held wrong it will break under its own weight. Marble is also quite porous and therefore easily stained. Old house owners often try to install marble mantels or vanities with modern glue. The glue soaks through the marble, leaving a permanent stain. Plaster of paris is the proper cement for marble.

The cost to purchase an original Victorian mantel depends upon how ornate the mantel is and what it is made of. Simple wood mantels often cost no more than $100. The going price for most ornate Victorian marble, oak or mahogany mantels is $500 to $800. A very ornate hand-carved mantel can command a price above $1,000.

In addition to salvaged Victorian mantels, new mantels are being manufactured from which you can select. *Decorators Supply Company* at 3610 South Morgan, Chicago makes a line of fourteen different wood mantels ranging in price from $300 to $500, and several models are Victorian in style. Further, most of the large building supply outlets distribute a line of simple wood mantels. *Midwest Jobbers*, the largest millwork distributor in the Chicago area, sells a line of six simple wood mantels ranging in price from $100 to $350 and available at most local building supply and lumber retailers.

Some of the simple wood mantels that retail for $200 or more are not difficult to construct if you have some carpentry ability. A wood fireplace mantel is mostly straight lines with no intricate components. Most of the mantel ornamentation can be constructed of stock wood moulding available at any lumberyard in red oak, birch or pine.

At about the turn of the century gas fireplaces became popular for their superior heating abilities and cleaner operation. (A fireplace designed for a gas unit is easy to recognize as its throat and firebox are small compared to a wood-burning fireplace.) Present-day owners do not find the romance in a gas fireplace that they find in a wood-burning fireplace, but experts recommend against converting a gas fireplace to a wood-burning fireplace. Even if there is room to install a larger firebox, the original gas flue will probably not be adequate.

Not all old houses have fireplaces, though most owners desire them. Building a traditional masonry fireplace will cost thousands of dollars, mainly because a support foundation must be poured. There are, however, steel fireplaces on the market which are much less expensive but just as good. Built of double steel hulls, these fireboxes are lightweight and can be placed on a wood floor anywhere in a house, with a traditional mantel placed in front to look Victorian. The biggest installation problem is usually in finding a convenient location for running new flue (also metal rather than brick) to the roof. Under various brand names such as Heatilator and Majestic, steel fireboxes cost from $500 to $600, and of course new mantel and installation costs must be added to the total.

STAIRCASES

A severely dilapidated staircase is something of a rarity in old Chicago area houses. In fact, in many abused old houses the staircase is the only interior element that has not decayed or been stripped during a "modernization." With the passing of eighty years, however, wood staircase steps (treads) may have shrunk and become loose. Loose treads are easy to rectify by driving wedges between the tread and the staircase stringers (a stringer is the diagonal structural beam that supports the stairs). However, getting into staircases to install wedges often entails tearing off plaster and lath from the underside of the staircase or removing large areas of wood trim that could be damaged in the process. Tearing out plaster or risking damage to wood trim is a high price to pay just to eliminate the irritation of a creaking step. If the entire staircase sags or bounces, a stringer is probably damaged, in which case the staircase will have to be rebuilt.

While structually unsound staircases are an uncommon problem, missing or damaged staircase parts, especially balusters or treads, is not. If the staircase does not require ornate replacements, that is if the balusters are a softwood and in a simple design, and if there are a large number of balusters to be replaced, probably the cheapest approach is to purchase an entire new set of stock balusters. The large millworks that supply retail lumberyards offer several baluster designs, ranging in price from $3 to $8 apiece. If just a few simple balusters need to be replaced, usually any carpenter with a lathe can turn them for you.

For more complicated designs, there are several woodworking firms in the Chicago area that specialize in building new staircases and that will take custom orders for replacement balusters. These are *Terp* at 2427 W. Irving Park in Chicago, *Norberg* at 3368 N. Elston in Chicago, *Interior Stairworks* in Lyons, and several others. However, as is usually true in the carpentry and wood products business, during the warm weather months these firms often have more business than they can handle, so they may not accept small custom orders. On the other hand, during the cold weather slack period most will readily accept small orders and at more reasonable prices.

Actually, almost all stair builders subcontract their baluster work to woodturners. The woodturner with the most patronage from stair builders in the Chicago area seems to be *Benteler* at 1436 N. Keating in Chicago, but there are other woodturners that accept small orders for balusters, such as *Bonnett* at 2239 N. Kimball in Chicago and *Pagel* at 2534 S. Western in Chicago. Whether you should contract a woodturner, a stair builder or a general carpenter to supply replacement balusters depends upon whether a professional is needed to install them. A woodturner will only fashion the baluster, he will not perform any work on the staircase in place. Also, a stair builder or carpenter will work on rail and tread repair or replacement while woodturners usually will not.

In some old houses, balusters are hardwood turned or carved in a more than simple design. Replacement of ornate balusters demands the skill of an expert wood craftsman and costs significantly more ($20 apiece is a frequent price, and some balusters in a rope design can cost $100 apiece). An artisan who specializes in the repair of antique wood furniture may be what you need. The best way to locate such craftsmen is to inquire with community organizations in old neighborhoods, organizations that have restored a landmark house, or dealers in antique furniture.

Not all old houses have ornate and appealing staircases, of course, and it often makes sense to remove the old staircase and replace it with a new one of modern design. One of the most popular stairways for a modern interior is the ornamental iron spiral stairway. Iron stairways are relatively inexpensive, efficient in their use of space, and easy to install. An ornamental iron spiral stairway with oak treads (12 feet high, 6 feet across) costs about $1,200. Several ironworks in Chicago will custom-make iron stairways and several companies, such as *Woodbridge* on N. Clybourn in Chicago, manufacture and market iron stairways nationally.

WALLS AND CEILINGS

If you stroll along the sidewalks in certain old neighborhoods of Chicago and glance in the front windows of the houses along the way, in building after building you will see interior walls of exposed brick. During the late Sixties and early Seventies, tearing plaster off interior walls and sandblasting the underlying brick became so popular in building rehabilitations that the very word "rehab" implied exposed brick walls. Many developers even installed interior brick walls in frame houses.

As a style of interior decoration for an old house, there is nothing wrong with exposed brick, except perhaps that it is now something of a cliché. However, before you start tearing out your old plaster walls to expose the underlying brick, you should consider the following: plaster is an excellent thermal insulator. Removing plaster from the inside of an exterior wall is likely to increase heating costs. Plaster is also an excellent absorber of sound, especially in the harsh high frequencies. Finally, plaster in a Victorian house is honest. Developers and rehabbers have often promoted exposed brick as "rustic" or "Victorian." Whether exposed brick walls are rustic is moot, but certainly they are not Victorian.

It is an extremely rare old house that does not need some wall repair or replacement during a renovation. If walls have not been damaged by age and past abuse, they likely will be damaged during repair or installation of heating ducts, chimneys, electrical lines, and so forth. In many rehabilitations, especially the gut- and-rebuild types, work begins by tearing out all the original plaster and lath walls and ceilings. After all the new service systems have been installed and any structural changes or repairs completed, new walls and ceilings of sheetrock (otherwise called drywall or gypsum wallboard) are usually installed in lieu of plaster and lath.

Drywall long ago superseded plaster and lath because it is cheaper and easier to apply. Sheetrock costs about 15 cents per square foot for

⅝-inch board, and the cost to have a contractor install it is 40 to 70 cents per square foot. It requires less skill to nail a plaster board to a wall, tape the joints and bead the corners than it does to apply plaster to lath. Be that as it may, only plumbers have earned more animosity than drywall contractors from owners of renovated houses. Installing new drywall in an old house can be tricky. Foundations settle unevenly, so that floors are not always level, and accurate fitting of the board is difficult (the board is square but the house is not). More than a few disappointed old house owners have ended up with crooked walls that display conspicuous taping at board joints and corners. Here again, shop for a reliable contractor.

In old houses with plaster walls and ceilings in generally good repair (plaster firmly attached to lath and lime not leached out) there is still likely to be much patching due to damage from electrical or plumbing repair. A good plasterer can make patches relatively fast and, if you have all the patching done at the same time, inexpensively. Nevertheless, minor wall and ceiling repairs are well within the capacity of the reasonably handy do-it-yourselfer, and since the materials are very inexpensive, money can be saved. Consult the home repair books and try out your skill in an inconspicuous place. If you flub the job, the only serious damage will be to your ego.

If you do attempt your own repair, beware of using patching materials that are not waterproof in bathrooms and kitchens. Moisture quickly attacks ordinary sheetrock or taping compound and makes a mess of the repair. In areas that are likely to get damp, only waterproof plasterboard and taping compound should be used.

While many building owners have repaired their walls and ceilings successfully simply by following instructions in repair or restoration publications, the repair of ornamental plaster is something else again. This work requires the skill of a professional, and the consequences of a botched job could be grave. The Chicago Plastering Institute at 5859 W. Fullerton in Chicago has a referral list of plasterers who can repair or replace ornamental plaster, but it is usually better to seek referrals from community groups or other old house owners where there is some proof of acceptable work.

Any original ornamental plaster in an old house can be duplicated if there is at least one small section of intact plaster from which a rubber latex mold can be formed. Where the original ornamental plaster has been totally destroyed, a plasterer can install new cast plaster. Most plaster contractors in the Chicago area use plaster casts purchased from *Decorators Supply Corporation* at 3610 S. Morgan in Chicago, and perusing a *Decorators Supply* catalog is a good way of becoming familiar with the range of ornamental plaster styles. The cost to have new ornamental plaster installed will depend upon the delicacy of the ornament design and the amount of work contracted. The more delicate the ornament design, the greater the expense, and the more plaster work contracted, the lower the unit cost. A cast cornice of standard design might cost $5 per foot, which is significantly less expensive than new hardwood cornice mouldings. To install all-new ornamental plaster (cornice, rosette and rope moulding) in a 400 square foot room, a reasonable cost estimate would be $1,000.

Cast ornamental plaster manufacture and installation is pretty much the province of artisans and professional contractors. There are, however, several kinds of ersatz ornaments in plastic on the market that house owners can install themselves. Most plastic reproductions of original Victorian features look like plastic reproductions, completely unworthy of use in a Victorian house, but the fidelity of ersatz ornamental plaster is excellent, and it is much cheaper than the real thing. Two firms, *Focal Point* at 1760 S. Roswell Rd., Marietta, Georgia 30060 and *W.H.S. Lloyd Co.* at 979 Third Avenue, Suite 1022, New York, N.Y. 10022, have been selling plastic ornaments for some years and will send a brochure of their products upon request. Ceiling cornices average about $3 per foot, while ceiling medallions range from $10 to $140.

Authentic Victorian interiors are often too dark and cluttered for modern tastes. Victorians filled all possible interior space with ornamentation. Notice in this Victorian interior that even the fireplace box when not in use is covered with a heavily embellished picture frame.

WOODWORK AND TRIM

Stripping and refinishing woodwork, like filling plaster cracks, is a project zealous old house owners often have underway almost before their signatures have dried on the Sale Contract. With good advice and the right tools, even a complete novice can get good results.

Often renovators assume that the only woods worth stripping are the hardwoods — oak, maple, walnut and mahogany, and that the only reason to do it is to expose the natural wood underneath. Actually, any decorative feature, whether plaster, metal, or soft wood, should be stripped and revarnished or repainted if the build-up is heavy. Once paint is removed from plaster ceiling medallions, metal newel posts, pine trim around doors, and so on, the original lines and forms become much more conspicuous and appealing. Similarly, varnish on hardwood trim will darken over time, becoming so opaque that the underlying wood appears jet black in color. Such wood appears unattractive and even depressing, which may be why people often painted over otherwise attractive hardwood trim. The beauty of darkened hardwood can be restored by removing old varnish and refinishing the wood. Considering that there are far more decorative objects than just hardwood trim to be stripped in a typical old house and that it often requires several applications of stripper to remove all paint, paint stripping becomes a much larger expense of both time and money than people generally bargained for.

There are many ways to strip paint and varnishes, and no one way is clearly superior to the others. Stripping with lye is an ancient method, fast, effective and relatively cheap. Several old house owners have made dip tanks for lye by splitting 50 gallon barrels in half lengthwise, then stripping their wood by dipping. (But here again, if the wood starts to crack or splinter as you try to remove it, cease and desist.) While lye is an effective paint stripper, it is also an effective wood destroyer. It does not distinguish between paint and wood, and if wood is held in lye too long, it will be destroyed.

Other old house owners achieve good results by using trisodium phosphate. Trisodium phosphate is effective in stripping most paints, it can be used with wood in place, and it is relatively inexpensive. It is also illegal in Chicago because it is so toxic. Nevertheless, like handguns, trisodium phosphate is readily available across city limits. There are also dozens of proprietary chemical strippers on the market which usually contain methylene chloride, benzol, alcohol, mineral spirits and other materials in sundry combinations. These commercial strippers are usually safe to use on any wood, but they are not always effective for all paints.

Another common method of stripping paint from wood or metal is by using a small handheld propane torch. The heat causes the paint to blister and pull away from the wood or metal in a film. If you use this method, have a fire extinguisher within arm's reach. Similarly, powerful hand-held hot air blowers are often used to soften layers of old shellac or varnish so that they can be removed with a putty knife. However, it is easy to scorch wood by holding heat on it for too long.

With so many different strippers and methods, probably the best approach for an inexperienced renovator is to talk to several house owners who have previously stripped woodwork and to consult one of the many how-to publications on wood stripping and refinishing. Certainly there will not be a consensus on any one method, but the more information you garner, the less likely you will be to make mistakes. One old house owner stripped the paint from one side of an interior oak door and left it in its frame. The exposed wood absorbed moisture and expanded in the frame until pressure caused the door to fracture. Such a mistake could have been avoided with some study on wood refinishing. Before committing much money to any one method or commercial brand of stripper, it is wise to test-strip a small area in an inconspicuous place to be sure you are satisfied with the product and your technique.

Although most old house owners do their own paint stripping, you do have the option of removing your painted woodwork and taking it to a professional stripper. Professional strippers with large dip tanks can work faster, and on some wood, such as carved balusters, do a more thorough job. If the built-up paint is thick, a professional stripper can actually be cheaper. Of course, professional paint strippers have been known to damage wood, so it is important to seek recommendations.

In many old houses doors have brass hardware, such as hinges, knobs, handles, plates and so forth that need stripping as well. Generally the same commercial chemical strippers that remove paint from wood will restore brass. However, some brass may have become stained or irreversibly tarnished. If so, it can usually be saved by replating. Silversmiths who specialize in refinishing small metal objects can usually replate brass hardware for a reasonable fee. There are several platers in the Chicago area who are experienced in brass replating: *Gilbertson Inc.* and the *House of William*, both on South Wabash in Chicago, *Albar-Wilmette* in Wilmette, Illinois, *Art Metal Finishers* at 6741 N. Clark, Chicago, *Junk Man Antiques* at 2154 N. Halsted, Chicago and *Custom Metal Polishing* at 1750 N. Campbell, Chicago.

Like stripping paint, refinishing wood can be done in many ways. It can be restained a dark or a light shade, it can be antiqued or treated by a traditional method such as graining, where a wood grain pattern is painted on the wood. Some people still use beeswax on their woodwork, while others prefer the long-lasting but glossy polyurethane finishes. Again, probably the best approach is to examine as much refinished woodwork in different styles as you can, and then decide which style and refinishing technique is most appealing. Then refinish a small area of wood in an inconspicuous place to be assured that the wood will look the way you expect and want it to.

Besides stripping and refinishing, interior woodwork may need replacing if it has been damaged or torn out during a modernization. The usual woodwork found in old houses includes stairs, mantels,

wainscoting, ceiling cornices, baseboards, chair rails, fretwork, spindling, window and door trim or jambs and, in some very ornate
houses, coffered ceilings. Most frequently in need of repair are the
various mouldings. There are manifold types and sizes of wood
mouldings, from simple quarter rounds to intricate crowns, many
available at lumberyards. Carpenters and contractors who specialize
in old house restoration can repair or fabricate new woodwork, but
if you are capable of installing new woodwork yourself, there are
dozens of places in the Chicago area that can make it. Besides millworks, such as *Waldbilling* at 4249 N. Elston or *Dettmers* at 920 W.
North Ave., there are several wood craftsmen who accept small custom orders — *Woodwares* at 2632 N. Lincoln Ave. and *Parenti and
Raffaelli* at 525 N. Noble in Chicago are just two. Fine cabinet makers and custom furniture makers often fabricate house woodwork
when they are not overwhelmed with cabinet work. *Custom Furniture* at 3454 N. Southport, Chicago, *Woodcraft Shop* at 1336 Maple,
Evanston and *Cabinetry & Design,* 625 Madison, Evanston are several
of many. Craftsmen who restore antique furniture, such as *Dovetail
Woodworks,* 6408 N. Campbell, Chicago, also sometimes do custom
woodwork. To order custom woodwork, you should have a good
print with accurate dimensions or a sample that the craftsman can
use as a guide.

In addition, many paint strippers and salvage shops sell salvaged
woodwork, especially door trim and interior shutters. Check such
places as *Speedy Strippers,* 2546 N. Halsted, *Sunset Strippers,* 3433 N.
Halsted, *Just Everything* on N. Lincoln or the *Renovation Source* on
N. Southport.

FLOORS

The last, or one of the last, projects undertaken in an interior renovation is the refinishing or replacement of wood floors. The unappealing floor coverings usually found in neglected old houses — paint,

linoleum, tile and carpets — do serve a purpose. They protect the underlying wood floor from any further damage during the renovation. Refinishing wood floors at the outset of the interior renovation subjects them to plaster debris, chemical solvents, heavy foot traffic, and other punishments best avoided.

Stripping floors of old coverings and refinishing the wood is another project that almost any house owner can handle himself. Yet quite a few people who have sanded and refinished their floors would hire a professional if they had to do it again. Sanding and stripping wood floors is an unpleasant task, dirty and frustrating because rental sanding equipment is not usually as efficient as a professional's, especially edgers for sanding the floor near base boards. Nevertheless, sanding or stripping wood floors is a drudgery often accepted by old house owners. It may be unpleasant, but it is not particularly difficult. Floor sanders can be rented from dozens of stores throughout the Chicago area. The sanding is simple — wood is sanded with the grain, never across the grain. Parquet floors which have closely-set inlaid wood can be difficult to sand without crossing grain somewhere. Some people try using solvent removers on parquet floors; others get down on their hands and knees to hand-sand the inlaid wood. If a professional sander is going to be used, care should be taken to assure that the contractor is competent with parquet floors. *Anderson-Ross* is well known for parquet floor refinishing, but there are several other firms that will sand parquet.

Removing old linoleum from wood floors can be as onerous as removing paint. If the linoleum cannot be pulled off, it may be necessary to resort to using a hand-held propane torch. Heat will melt linoleum so that it can be scraped off the floor with a stiff scraper. Another approach is to use a chlorinated-hydrocarbon solvent to dissolve the linoleum. The first approach seems more popular because dissolved linoleum can be a real mess to deal with.

How a wood floor is refinished is, again, purely a matter of taste and preference. Floors can be stained in light or dark shades. They can be finished with traditional shellac, conventional varnishes, newer quick-dry varnishes, penetrating sealers or polyurethanes. Each finish has its advantages and drawbacks in regard to wear resistance, yellowing, drying time, ease of application and removal. Polyurethanes were popular initially for their long-wearing qualities, but many people find the high sheen of polyurethane unattractive. Again, probably the best approach for evaluating floor finishes is to poll other old house owners for their experiences and to examine a variety of finished floors.

In old houses that have been neglected for a long time, floor damage goes beyond a mere build-up of old paint, linoleum, carpet or tile. When wood floors are continually subjected to water from leaking roofs or rotted window sash, they will permanently discolor to black and eventually rot. If the stain is deep into the wood, it cannot be removed by sanding. It will have to be replaced. Wood flooring is one building material of the Victorian era still commonly used in new buildings. There are several dozen floor retail outlets and installation firms that sell wood floors, including hardwood, softwood and parquet. Most major lumberyards sell a line of wood flooring, some of which is appropriate for old houses. New wood flooring starts at about $3 per square foot. If floor damage is limited to one area, rather than buy new flooring some old house owners have replaced damaged planks in a frequently-used room with intact planks from a room that is seldom used. Other old house owners have discovered that the subflooring under the damaged hardwood is an undamaged pine that, when refinished, looks appealing. And of course if the old wood floor is no longer attractive, there is no reason why new carpeting cannot be laid over the old floor.

9

The Exterior Appearance

Attending to the external appearance of an old house is usually the last concern in a typical renovation. In neighborhoods where regeneration is just beginning, people often leave their building's appearance unattended years after the interior renovation is complete as a defensive ploy — a rundown exterior will not betray expensive interior contents to burglars. Still, most owners eventually want their building to look as appealing as possible.

But what makes a building attractive? As the old saw goes, "beauty is in the eye of the beholder." There are no absolutes to good appearance or good taste. Nevertheless, the human mind responds predictably to certain colors, forms or designs; much of architectural study is based on the belief that people share certain principles of physical attractiveness.

To be attractive, a building must be in proportion. That is, the ratio of vertical to horizontal elements must be correct, whether those elements are perceived as the basic dimensions of the building or as elements of its facade, such as windows or doors. A building whose vertical elements overwhelm the horizontal, or vice versa, will look peculiarly out of balance; it will not please.

Besides proportion, an attractive building must possess balance. If too many elements — windows, doors, porches and so on — are on

In the name of building improvement, people have filled in window openings with brick and glass block, replaced Victorian doors with flush doors, and covered porches with cheap aluminum awnings. The result is not an improvement.

one side of a front facade, it will look out of balance, esthetically displeasing.

Scale is another basic element of design. Scale, a form of proportion, is the relationship between building size, or perceived size, and the human being. A building, door or porch may have good proportion, but if it is out of scale with the human element, people will have a feeling that something is wrong. A building out of scale may evoke sensations of insignificance or awkwardness; it will seem unattractive even though it is identical to a building that is attractive in correct human scale.

A building must be in proper scale, balance and proportion, and it also must be honest. If the building elements do not relate properly or honestly to each other, a sense of confusion will be engendered — a feeling that something is not right. A building must look like what it is. A wood building should look like a wood building, and a brick building should look like a brick building. And in general, architectural styles should not be mixed. A colonial Georgian-style doorway will look very peculiar on a Victorian Chicago facade.

Nor can a building's appearance be judged in isolation, for a building is inseparably part of its block and neighborhood. Like a building, a neighborhood or block must have good proportion, balance and scale to be attractive, and if one building disturbs the neighborhood's proportion, scale or balance, the beauty of the entire neighborhood will be marred. Everyone has visited at one time or another a neighborhood of nice houses all in harmony except for one that is painted a bright loud off-color. Paint of course can easily be changed for the better; there are worse examples of ill-considered exterior changes that upset the unity and harmony of a neighborhood.

There is no shortage throughout Chicago of well-intentioned but unsuccessful attempts by old house owners to improve the appearance of their houses. Window openings have been added, reduced, or increased, porches have been removed and added, ornamentation has been removed and every conceivable material — asphalt, vinyl, masonite, perma-stone, cedar shingles and planks, aluminum — has been used as false siding. How should you as the owner of an old house approach the exterior renovation of your building? The guiding principle should be to restore the building's appearance as nearly to the original condition as possible. As architects and preservationists are fond of saying, "Do not destroy a building's integrity."

ROOFS

Roofs were rarely used for esthetic display in Victorian Chicago. Flat roofs were completely hidden by parapet walls, and pitched roofs, unless there was an unobstructed side view, were little more conspicuous. Roofs in Victorian Chicago were generally treated as a practical necessity.

Of course there were exceptions. Roofs of colorful slate or tile were meant to be seen, and so was the French Mansard roof, a style of slate roof especially popular in the 1870s and 1880s. Shingles on Mansard roofs were often laid out in pattern — a band of square shingles, then a band of diamond-shaped or pentagonal shingles, then another band of square shingles. Mansard roofs wider at the bottom than at the top often had shingles that became incrementally larger from top to bottom, a design perhaps best described as "reptilian scale" because it resembles the skin of some snakes and lizards.

Despite the beauty of Victorian tile and slate roofs, most have not fared well through the years. The tile and slate, if properly maintained, will last for centuries, but the underlying roofing felt deteriorates after about thirty years. Many past owners simply tore the slate or tile off their roofs and recovered with inexpensive asphalt roll when the roofing felt needed replacing. If the roof was not prominently visible nothing was really lost, but if the roof was a major element in the building's esthetic design, then the loss is serious. Similarly, houses with red, green or gray ceramic tile roofs will lose appeal if the colorful three-dimensional tile is replaced with asphalt.

If the roof's appearance is important to a building's overall design, then original roofing material should be retained or restored if at all possible.

There is no cheap way around it — repairing, preserving or restoring slate or tile roofs is expensive. If the roofing felt is shot, all the slate or tile must be removed, new roofing felt laid down and finally the original slate or tile reinstalled. Such a repair is labor intensive and expensive because slate and tile is tricky to work with. In addition, if the slate is not common black slate, matching original color is expensive because replacement slate will have to come from the original slate quarry. One Chicago area resident restoring a mansion with a red slate roof discovered that the colored slate came from only one quarry and new slate would cost $935 per square (100 square feet) as compared to only $30 per square for asphalt shingle, excluding installation. He needed three squares of replacement slate. He bought it.

Ordinary slate costs roughly $175 to $200 per square depending upon the type and size. A single common slate shingle 16″ by 8″ costs a dollar. In general, repairing a slate or clay tile roof will cost three to four times more than repairing with asphalt shingle. There are still a number of roofing contractors in and around Chicago who can do excellent work on slate and tile roofs. Community organizations in older neighborhoods are usually familiar with these roofing contractors, and they are the best place to seek a reference. To purchase individual slate or clay tile shingles, the main supply outlet in Chicago is *Nebrich* at 1645 Wolfram.

Few renovators themselves try major roof recoverings or restorations with slate or clay tile shingle. These materials are very brittle, and if applied incorrectly they will soon crack and break. Still, small repairs by building owners are not uncommon. There is a standard repair procedure described in most "how-to" books (list in back of book) for replacing a single slate shingle that has broken off. The only special tool needed is a roofing nail cutter, which can easily be fashioned. At the very least, house owners can accomplish general maintenance repair of cracked slate or clay tile shingles. If a crack develops, it can be temporarily repaired with asphalt roofing compound. But you must never climb on a slate or clay tile roof without providing some means of distributing your body weight over a wide area of roof. Professional roofers use a roofing ladder. The do-it-yourself house owners must be at least as solicitous of brittle roof covering.

Ceramic or glazed tile, called variously field tile or pantile, is as much a problem to repair or restore as slate or clay tile. Glazed tile roofs on turrets or towers may be beyond hope of repair. The tile on these roofs was usually custom-ordered when the house was built, and finding replacement tile may be next to impossible. There is still a company that will make new custom tile, but the entire roof will have to be recovered if the colors are to match. Field tile on flat planes is usually more easily repaired or restored. Replacement tile can be obtained at *Nebrich's* or through a roofing contractor who specializes in tile.

Restoring or preserving a tile or slate roof is important, but if the expense is simply beyond your means, then at the very least avoid installing an asphalt roof in bright conspicuous colors. Asphalt shingle in bright reds or greens on roofs meant to be tiled will only draw attention to the inappropriate roof covering. If you have to use asphalt shingle instead of tile, then plain inobtrusive black is the proper color.

By the same token, if a roof was not meant to be visually prominent, do not try to make it so. Drawing attention to the roof will divert attention from the exterior elements that were supposed to make the building's visual statement. The most frequent mistake in this regard is using an improper roofing material, usually the new imitation wood shingle. Wood shingle was a standard roofing material during the Colonial era. Wood shingles belong on Eastern Colonials, rural farmhouses or instant-rustic suburban roofs, but not on nineteenth-century Chicago buildings.

One roof covering that combines practicality with beauty is metal.

Metal has been used as a roof covering throughout America since the Colonial era, though rarely in Chicago. (The landmark Hull House on the Chicago Circle Campus has a metal roof, as do several other old lakefront mansions. Probably the best metal roof in Chicago is on the old Wrigley Mansion at Lake View and Arlington Place.) Metal roofs are of several types — copper, lead-coated copper and terne. Terne is an alloy of 80% lead and 20% tin, usually used as a coating over steel sheet. Needless to say, a metal roof, especially one of copper, will be many times more expensive to install than an asphalt roof. On the other hand, metal roofs are the most permanent, maintenance-free roofs available, while asphalt usually lasts no more than twenty years. The permanence of a metal roof is especially desirable if the interior plasterwork immediately under the roof is valuable. After all, a roof leak is most frequently discovered when interior plaster becomes soaked and damaged. A metal roof provides peace of mind. Installing metal roofs is not a lost art; many roofing contractors in Chicago still work with metal, so there should be little difficulty in locating a reputable contractor.

Although Chicago Victorian roofs were rarely designed to be ornate, Victorian-era architects and builders did use one roof embellishment that old house renovators might consider — ornamental iron roof cresting. Some of the best examples of ornamental iron cresting can be seen on the Kimball House in the Prairie Avenue Historical District, on the old McCormickville mansion at Dearborn and Elm that now serves as Biggs Restaurant, and on the companion house immediately west of the landmark Dewes House at Wrightwood and Hampton Court. Roof cresting is a decorative wrought ironwork usually four to fifteen inches in height that runs across the top ridge of a house. It is especially effective when it embellishes a building's porch and bay front as well as the roof. When it was placed on sloped roof ridges, it was often called a Widow's Walk. Sometimes cresting was a simple lattice design; other times it was an intricate and convoluted pattern. Esthetically, it provides some hori-

Ornamental iron cresting along a roof ridge and across a front bay.

zontal definition to building form. While its lack or loss is not likely to destroy a building's proportion, cresting can lend an air of distinction, and present-day house owners might give it consideration.

Ornamental iron roof cresting can still be fashioned today, though most local ironsmiths have never heard of it. Any ironsmith who can fashion a decorative iron window or door guard can make ornamental iron roof cresting if a customer has a good blueprint or a piece of cresting for reproduction. One ironsmith in Chicago who has done work in this specialty is Bob Mueller at 3631 N. Cicero. The cost depends upon the complexity of the design. A simple design would likely cost from $12 to $15 per foot, or several hundred dollars for a typical old house.

PORCHES AND PORTICOES

It is the exterior design elements — the porches, porticoes, balconies, windows, doors and cornices — that give an old house its charm and appeal. Without these features a house would be nothing more than a large, monotonous box. Nineteenth-century Chicago builders frequently embellished the facades of their buildings with window and door trim, cornices and small porches. Large veranda-like porches are uncommon in older inner city neighborhoods, especially on masonry houses. Balconies are rarer yet.

To nineteenth-century Chicago architects and builders, large porches and balconies were pointless. Chicago is a northern city with inclement weather half the year and industrial pollution, especially a century ago, all year. Consequently domestic life in late nineteenth-century Chicago was oriented inwards, not outwards. The only purpose for a porch in Chicago was to protect people passing into the building from inclement weather. In many instances the porch covering was nothing more than a small canopy cantilevered from the building facade, and it was not uncommon for houses to be built without any porch or door covering, Chicagoans being a hardy breed.

The porch was often the most embellished section of a building exterior. Notice how attractive simple lattice balusters can be. Certainly wrought iron could do no more for this Victorian house.

Perhaps the most striking example of inward orientation is the Glessner mansion at 18th and Prairie Avenue, built between the Stockyards and Illinois Central Railroad. Considering the noxious breezes of the area, it is understandable that Glessner had his architect, Henry H. Richardson, design a house around an interior courtyard. The Glessner House is devoid of all exterior decoration, and except for the doors and a few window openings it could be mistaken for a fortress. Old houses with veranda-like porches are far more common in neighborhoods that were rural or suburban in the late nineteenth century, such as Lake View, Morgan Park, Austin or Evanston.

But even if the utilitarian role of porches in the city was slight, they were often the vehicle for much of the adornment used on building exteriors. Intricate wood spindling, wood moulding, fretwork, sawnwood ornaments and wood lattice were often used to bridge the space between porch columns or as part of the rails. The columns were usually turned in popular baluster shapes. Besides being richly decorated and visually interesting in their own right, porches were an essential element in establishing scale, proportion, and balance for the entire building. For this reason, the original look of a house cannot be maintained if the architectural style or proportion of the porch is altered.

One unfortunate vestige of the era of house "modernization" is the practice of putting a new porch on an old house. The two most frequent disfigurements are replacing an old portico with a new aluminum awning and replacing original porch support columns with new ornamental iron supports. Because an aluminum porch covering is rarely as large as the wood covering it replaces, it cannot be congruent with the building's proportion. Moreover, the great natural advantages of aluminum, its light weight and flexibility, lead to esthetic effects that are the exact opposite of those achieved with wood. Likewise the popular practice of replacing original wooden porch columns with ornamental iron is certain to produce an esthetic disaster. Retail merchants from small iron works to giants like

"New Orleans" style ironwork is attractive, but it is too light and fragile for heavy Victorian architecture. The ironwork porch columns on this house are barely visible up close. From a distance they seem to disappear altogether, and the porch looks unsupported.

Sears and Montgomery Ward have been touting "New Orleans" style ornamental iron porch columns and railings as a means of adding some appeal to old houses. Viewed by itself, this "New Orleans" ironwork, with its delicate and lacy designs, is very attractive. Nevertheless, it is totally inappropriate to most Victorian houses, just as the light and airy architecture of the French Quarter in New Orleans would hardly be "improved" if residents there replaced their delicate ironwork with Victorian columns.

Removing aluminum awnings is relatively easy and inexpensive, but replacing porch columns is not. Two general types of porch columns were used in Chicago during the Victorian era, large diameter hollow columns in a classical style, and solid wood turned columns. Hollow classical porch columns came both smooth and fluted, with an Ionic or Corinthian capital or a plain round cap. Replacing a column with an Ionic or Corinthian capital is difficult, because it it no longer a stock mill item. Duplicating it requires the services of a wood craftsman and is therefore too expensive for most house owners. However, the hollow column with a simple cap is still a stock item distributed by *Midwest Jobbers* of St. Charles and sold at most Chicago lumberyards. Large diameter wood columns do not come cheap, however. A typical plain 10-inch diameter column ten feet high costs around $150, fluted columns generally cost an additional thirty dollars. Occasionally some original classical columns show up in antique-salvage shops such as *Just Everything,* 2965 N. Lincoln, *The Renovation Source,* 3512 N. Southport, or *Antiques 'n' Things,* 1323 W. Webster in Chicago. But the first place to look is in your own attic, basement, and garage. Several house owners have discovered that the past owner who removed the columns stored them away instead of disposing of them.

Solid wood porch columns were usually made from a 5″ x 5″ square pine post with the top and bottom two feet or so left square and the middle section turned in various rounded shapes. Quite often the square sections were embellished by chamfering and bevel-

Inexpensive and easily made square porch posts are an acceptable substitute for missing original posts of solid wood in turned designs.

ing. Since pine porch columns are not stock lumberyard items, they will have to be custom-ordered from a millwork. There are several small millworks throughout Chicago that readily accept small custom orders for old house renovations, but most millworks subcontract this work to *Benteler & Sons* at 1436 N. Keating in Chicago, and they will accept orders directly from building owners. The cost of a replacement post will depend upon whether the square sections are chamfered or beveled, how intricate the turned design is, and of course the height of the post. Usually solid pine replacement posts average $150 to $300.

If the cost of professional work is prohibitive, an esthetically acceptable and relatively inexpensive way of replacing porch posts is to build square posts from stock lumberyard 2x6s, ¾-inch exterior plywood and standard moulding. A simple square post will not be as graceful as a solid pine turned post, but it will have the solid look appropriate to Victorian architecture.

Reconstructing an entire porch is a major operation that must be done with considerable caution; a design mistake here will be conspicuous. The safest approach is to try and make the porch look as it once did, and if the original design did not include a porch, it is probably unwise to add one because it will almost certainly look "stuck on."

WINDOWS AND DOORS

Just a short stroll along the streets of any old Chicago neighborhood will show how many different designs and styles were used for windows and doors. In spite of the variety, late nineteenth-century Chicago builders preferred certain basic designs. These were neither conceived in Chicago nor unique to Chicago, but perhaps they can be denominated a "Chicago style" because of their frequency in Victorian-era Chicago houses.

Glass block windows and concrete block porch supports profane this once-attractive masonry facade.

Basic window design is determined by the size, shape and number of panes in each window sash. In Colonial and Early American houses, windows usually had many small panes as a matter of necessity — primitive glass manufacturing methods made large panes very expensive. By the late nineteenth century, when most old Chicago buildings were constructed, large sheets of glass had become relatively inexpensive and the double-hung sash window had become commonplace (the double-hung sash window is the familiar window with a top sash that slides down on its track and a bottom sash that slides up on another track. The sash are kept in place either by springs or by counter-weights). Although small window panes were no longer necessary in Victorian Chicago, many Chicago builders continued to use them out of tradition.

On the other hand, the lack of small panes does not necessarily mean that the windows in an old house have been altered for the worse; the original design may well have called for large panes. Windows and window openings in old Chicago buildings have been frequent victims of the renovator who wants to "improve" his building's appearance, particularly during the "modernizations" of the Fifties and Sixties. Whether the windows have been made larger or smaller, the building's proportion and scale have likely been sacrificed. Repairing damaged window openings is moderately difficult, but easier if the window openings were made smaller than if they were made larger — it is generally easier to remove alien brick than to locate matching old brick. If matching brick cannot be obtained, repair scars will be evident, and you will have no choice but to paint the facade. In wood-frame houses, restoring window openings to their original proportion is not so difficult because there is no problem in matching facade materials.

While the redesign of window openings has been on the wane, too many recent renovations have disregarded the visual importance of window details. One current fad is to tear out everything in the window openings — mullions, frames, sash — and replace them with

one large non-opening sheet of thermopane glass. Such an alteration
will cause a major visual change, and not a benign change either.
Muntins and mullions are part of the detailing that adds interest to
a building's facade. (Muntins are narrow wood frames supporting
individual glass panes, while mullions are the larger frames that support and separate whole sash windows. Actually some authorities
use the words interchangeably.) Furthermore, the larger mullions
play an important role in establishing good building proportion. An
old house will have a more pleasing appearance if it possesses original
window sash in the full original window opening.

It can be difficult and expensive to restore original mullions and
sash because many old houses require large odd sizes no longer available at lumberyards. Custom sash can be ordered at several millworks in Chicago, but *Hohmeier* at 2011 W. Belmont, Chicago seems
to have garnered the most business in this specialty. To some, the expense of new custom-made sash and frames is not worthwhile, especially if the windows will rarely be opened after installation of
central air-conditioning. If the original sash windows are not going
to be restored, at the very least the original proportions of the window should be restored. There are far too many woe-begone old
houses throughout Chicago where a previous owner replaced the
original large sash with smaller standard-size sash and then filled the
void above the new window with stucco, brick or wood. Besides altering the building's proportions, the filled spaces usually appear unattractive and incongruous on the facade, especially when the reduced window opening leaves the original lintels ludicrously float-
ing several feet above the windows they are supposed to top. For an
old house to look as it was meant to, it is imperative that the original
window openings be filled in with glass; and if the original sash
windows are not going to be restored, then a frame of thermopane
glass is a tolerable alternative.

Thermopane does have practical advantages — the double-paned,
sealed glass is a good insulator, and it is resistant to break-ins by bur-

glars. Many renovators compromise by putting thermopane in first-floor windows while leaving the upper-floor windows in the original sash. A mass-produced product, thermopane is easily procured; just about every glass retail outlet is in this business. Thermopane comes clear and in various tints. In houses with a southern exposure, tinted glass can be used to reduce interior glare. However, while tinted glass for southern exposure makes sense, a very dark tint should be avoided. From even a short distance the dark glass appears totally opaque, as if someone had installed black sheet metal in all the window openings. Furthermore, dark colors tend to exaggerate the size of the window. Clear thermopane one inch thick for a 3′ x 5′ window costs approximately $100, while a heavily bronzed glass of the same size costs approximately $175.

Because sashless windows cannot be opened, people sometimes install thermopane in a frame that includes a small eyebrow window (an eyebrow window is a bottom-hinged, inward-opening window). These windows are a modern design not proper in old houses. If it is necessary to have windows that open in the front facade, full sash windows should be installed.

In regard to windows, perhaps the most common mistake made by owners of old houses is to install storm windows with shiny aluminum frames. Bright, space-age aluminum does not belong with Victorian architecture. Victorians painted their window frames black to give them depth, to give the windows the effect of being set into the facade. Shiny aluminum reverses the original design, so that the windows appear to project out of the facade. Furthermore, in sunshine the bright metal tends to catch a viewer's attention and draw it away from the rest of the facade.

There is nothing wrong with aluminum window frames per se, as long as the aluminum is not shiny. Aluminum frames can be purchased with a baked enamel covering in black or dark brown that does not conflict with the surrounding window frames. Some storm window suppliers charge several dollars extra for baked enamel win-

Useless shutters clutter the lovely facade of this Victorian row house.

dows, but many do not. Shop around until you find one of the latter. If shiny aluminum storm windows have already been installed, the only way to mute their effect is with paint. Several commercially available paints will adhere to aluminum, but none will adhere permanently. Repainting and touch-up will become a continuing responsibility.

Space-age aluminum does not belong with Victorian architecture, and neither do Colonial window shutters. In the Colonial era, shutters were not ornaments but safeguards protecting expensive windows from inclement weather. In fact, on many modest Colonial dwellings shutters were nothing more than large wood planks on hinges. With the advent of inexpensive large-pane glass and double-hung sash in the nineteenth century, shutters fell out of use, especially in Chicago. On Victorian buildings shutters look cluttered, and they draw attention away from the original ornaments. In many cases the shutters are obviously too large or too small ever to have been used as window covers. Many people like the look of window shutters, but if you are the owner of a Chicago Victorian house you should think twice before installing them.

Some old house owners encounter problems with curved glass in turret and tower windows. Windows in towers, turrets and rounded bay fronts usually were made with the same curve as the structure they were part of, giving the structure a fullness and unity of form. When the windows needed repair, house owners often took the expedient way out by replacing the curved windows with standard flat sash windows. The savings in repair money comes at the expense of the building's appearance. Flat windows in a round tower may not be hideous, but they are not beautiful, either. Unfortunately, repairing curved windows is expensive and replacing them is very expensive. Curved glass must be custom-formed at a factory, but just about any retail glass outlet can order it at approximately $200 for a typical window. Lexan, a transparent plastic, is used occasionally in lieu of curved plate glass in towers and turrets of old houses. Lexan can be bent to imitate original panes and is usually less expensive than replacement glass. The real expense occurs when the curved window frames and sash as well as curved glass must be replaced. If there are more than a couple of windows in need of replacement, the cost will quickly go to four figures.

Like windows and window openings, doors and doorways should correspond to the building facade in style and period. And again, the proper renovation approach is to try to preserve or restore the original door and doorway design. The most frequent "Chicago style" of the Victorian era was the double or split door with a single full-length transom directly above. The doors themselves were often solid wood embellished with wood carvings or panelled with geometric patterns of moulding. Equally popular were doors with panels of glass.

Since Chicago was built in marshy terrain, door openings were seldom placed near ground level. In fact Chicago's original street level was raised on several occasions, and builders, anticipating future street level increases, often constructed buildings with door openings quite high on the building facade. Because these elevated door openings are something of a Chicago tradition, it is advisable not to change them. Moreover, moving a door opening is very risky because doors and doorways comprise such a large part of a building's exterior appearance; moving them can easily distort the building's balance and proportion.

Still, many building owners have found a high doorway disadvantageous for a number of reasons. In some instances the steps and porch for a second level doorway obstruct first-floor windows and create a dark and gloomy first-floor interior. A second level front entrance can also cause annoying limitations to interior design, as conventional home layouts usually have a first-floor front entrance. Some of the shorter cottage-style houses with second level doorways look almost surreal, with their front entrance closer to the roof than to the ground. The best approach is to leave the old doorway trim in place and to fill the hole with glass. The new doorway should be constructed with trim in the same style and proportion as the original doorway, and of course only Victorian-style doors should be used.

The most frequent abuse of doors on old houses occurs through the use of styles and materials not found in nineteenth-century Chicago architecture. Victorian doors, even those with glass panels, were solid yet subdued in appearance. They were usually painted black or brown, and if left natural (unpainted) and varnished, the wood graining was not emphasized or made conspicuous. Yet owners of old city houses have often replaced Victorian doors with modern flush doors, which are usually bright yellow or orange in color with the wood grain emphasized. These cheap-looking modern doors are often fitted with small geometric panels of glass, a design never used in Victorian architecture.

In a similarly misguided effort to improve their buildings, many old house owners have removed both the original split doors and the transom window from their main entrances, replacing them with a single Colonial styled door and surrounding glass (sidelights and fanlights). Colonial doors on a Victorian house fail for the same reason that "New Orleans" ironwork porches do. Colonial doors and trim look light and fragile. They are too weak for the massive and heavy Victorian facade.

Perhaps the most egregious doorway blunder, however, is reducing a split door and transom window to a single door. This disfigures the building's proportion completely. To reestablish a pleasing proportion, the doorway must be restored. Constructing a new door frame for a double door and transom is not particularly difficult. A good carpenter or a house owner with some carpentry ability can build a door frame. If a more ornate frame with chamfering or beveling on the door jamb is desired, a custom frame will probably have to be ordered from a millwork experienced in restoration work, such as *Hohmeir* or *Waldbillig*.

Locating Victorian-style replacement doors can be frustrating. If you are fortunate, you may find the original doors stored away in the

A right way . . .

basement or attic. If not, most antique/salvage shops have an assortment of old doors — *Newberry's, 1524* S. Peoria, usually has a large supply of old doors while the *Renovation Source* usually has a selection of ornate salvaged doors. The large lumberyard and building supply outlets market a wide variety of exterior door styles, but few are appropriate for Victorian houses. The exception is the simple, six or eight square raised-panel pine door. This style was often used in the Victorian period. An exterior replacement door of this kind, made of good quality pine, will cost $150 or more, not expensive considering that it is you, the owner of the house, who must look at the door every time you enter or leave.

Besides choosing inappropriate door styles, renovators too often mar the appearance of doors and door trim by using improper building materials. Aluminum, as noted earlier, can detract from a building's appearance if it is obtrusively shiny and bright. But at least aluminum storm windows render a useful service as an insulator. Aluminum storm doors do not save much heat. In fact, a solid wood door with proper weatherstripping is insulation enough. Furthermore, aluminum storm doors are of little use in cities where people feel insecure with the front door open and guarded by nothing more than a screen. An aluminum storm door can be especially damaging to a building's appearance if it obstructs the original main door entirely from view, as some with panels of etched glass do. Aluminum doors are of little use and have no visual appeal on old houses.

Glass block is another twentieth-century building material incompatible with Victorian architecture. Glass block is often used for bathroom windows in commercial and industrial buildings, hardly the association one would want to evoke in a house. Many owners of old houses have replaced glass panes around doors with glass block because they fear that a burglar might enter by breaking the glass and reaching through to unlock the door from the inside. A better solution to this problem is to install a key-operated bolt on the inside of the door. If the key is kept out of reach, the door will be secure even if the glass is broken.

and a wrong way to remove a second-floor door opening.

While the Victorian house is not a proper setting for glass block, it is ideal for stained glass. Stained glass was widely used during the late nineteenth century even in relatively modest housing, and it is one of the amenities most cherished by present-day old house owners. Besides being colorful and attractive, stained glass illuminates the house interior with a mellow light, and throws interesting patterns of light and shadow which shift with the movement of the sun. One renovator with exceptionally attractive stained glass windows installed small floodlights on his building exterior to illuminate the stained glass panels at night. A stained glass window panel is unquestionably an object of art, and anyone restoring an old house should make every effort to save the original panels or, if they have been removed, to replace them.

To be accurate, stained glass is glass that has been painted and fired. Most colored glass in old buildings is leaded glass or cut glass, but "stained glass" seems to be the accepted term for any colored or bevelled glass. There is a lively commerce in stained glass in the Chicago area. Most antique stores carry some of it, and there are several retail establishments in Chicago that deal exclusively in stained glass windows and lamps. It is not cheap. The cost depends on the window size and intricacy of design: the more small pieces of glass or rondels in different colors and shapes or the more bevelling of the glass, the greater the value of the panel. Thus stained glass window panels can range in price from less than one hundred to over a thousand dollars. If a missing stained glass panel is of an odd size or shape, finding an antique replacement may prove impossible. The only solution to this problem is to pay a craftsman to reconstruct a new one.

Fortunately the art of stained glass repair and construction is still widely practiced. Chicago has a community of craftsmen actively working in this specialty, and several of the workshops sell repair materials such as leaded glass and metal colored epoxy, and conduct classes in stained glass construction for ambitious do-it-yourselfers. A new stained-glass panel designed and constructed from scratch is expensive. Here again, the more intricate the design the greater the

A house that has lost its cornice is a forlorn sight.

cost. Stained glass craftsmen are listed in the yellow pages under "Glass, Stained and Leaded." You can sometimes locate stained glass craftsmen at local outdoor art and craft fairs. Or read an issue of *Stained Glass* magazine, published by the Stained Glass Association of America. Each issue contains a directory of member studios (including several in the Chicago area), suppliers, and publications. You can find current and back issues of *Stained Glass* in the art section of the Chicago Cultural Center.

CORNICES

Generally speaking, the cornice was the largest single adornment of Victorian-era buildings in Chicago. The cornice defines the top of a facade. As most Chicago buildings of the late nineteenth century were built with a vertical emphasis, the cornice is the horizontal element that balances the building's vertical sight lines and provides pleasing proportion. The cornice is often the most attractive ornament on a building as well. Cornices are found in a wide variety of designs, shapes and materials. Some are set nearly flush to the building, while others project outward as much as three or four feet. Cornices may have simple straight lines, or they may be elaborately ornate with decorative brackets, dentils and stamped designs. They can be constructed of sheet metal, wood, stone, terra cotta or corbelled brick. On some buildings there may be more than one cornice — one at the very top of the parapet wall and a belt course usually three-fourths of the way up the facade.

A building which has lost its cornice is a forlorn sight, like a box without a lid. Unfortunately many once-handsome Chicago buildings have been stripped of their cornices, leaving the facade with a permanent scar of non-matching brick or piebald cement patching and spoiling the building's proportion to boot. Without a cornice to act as a horizontal counterweight to a building's vertical thrust, the pleasing balance between vertical and horizontal is utterly lost.

Without question, cornices are difficult and expensive to repair. In several recent renovations, cornice repair cost from five to ten thousand dollars. This is why so many building owners take the expedient option and tear their damaged cornices down. Nevertheless, if justice is to be done to a building, an honest effort should be made to preserve or restore the cornice as a crucial element in Victorian design.

To reduce cost, several house owners have done some cornice repair themselves. This is feasible when the cornice is metal, structurally sound, with holes no more than a foot across. The repair materials are asphalt roofing compound or liquid asphalt, and roofing membrane (this is a light, flexible roofing felt that is almost gauze-like in composition). Roofing membrane is placed over the hole and covered with trowelable asphalt compound or liquid asphalt. Layers of roofing membrane and asphalt are applied until the hole is filled. The asphalt and roofing membrane is flexible and can be molded and formed to follow the lines of the cornice without bulging. After several weeks of drying, the cornice and patches should be painted a dark color, black or brown.

Where large sections of the cornice are missing or badly eroded, the repair can only be made by replacement with new sheet metal. This is beyond the skill of most renovators, but finding a contractor to repair a metal cornice is no problem. As always, it is a matter of employing a reputable general contractor or roofer who specializes in old house repair.

One lament often heard is that cornice construction is a lost art. Not true; any cornice built in the late nineteenth century can also be built in the late twentieth century. What has been lost is the demand for new cornices. But even the intricate stamped metal ornaments, such as wreaths, shields, gargoyles, brackets and finials can be had from a firm in Wilton, Connecticut — *Kenneth Lynch & Sons.* A metalsmith who claims that no one makes stamped metal ornaments anymore is simply not up on the state of his art.

The cost to reconstruct a metal cornice will depend upon how large it is, what metal is used (tinsheet is much cheaper than copper) the height of the building and the intricacy of the cornice design. Replacing a large, ornate cornice in copper may run to five figures. However, a simple tinsheet cornice can be fashioned by many general contractors and roofing contractors. A more ornate and intricate replacement is usually the province of specialized metalshops. *Albert J. Wagner,* a long-time Chicago firm at 3762 N. Clark, and *Tappert Roofing,* at 5643 W. Irving Park in Chicago, have done much of the recent work on Chicago landmark buildings. There are three or four other firms in the area that can reconstruct elaborate metal cornices.

Most recent cornice replacements on smaller single-family houses have been wood reconstructions. The cost for a replacement cornice in wood is usually well under a thousand dollars, and the job can be accomplished by any good carpenter in the old house restoration field. If you are skilled in woodworking you can make a new cornice yourself, from treated wood or marine plywood. It should be installed so that water cannot penetrate the joint between cornice and building facade.

MASONRY AND STONE WALLS

For a masonry wall to look its best, it must look like a genuine masonry wall. In every old neighborhood there are monuments to the persuasiveness of a siding salesman and the ignorance of a building owner; masonry covered with false siding. What could be more ludicrous than a brick wall covered with false brick siding? The only way to make such a building attractive again is to tear the siding off, and this involves considerable risk. There is no way of knowing how badly the underlying brickwork is damaged until the siding has been removed. In the process of applying false siding, bricks may have been cracked or broken. Further, once the false siding has been torn off, several layers of paint may have to be removed before it can be decided whether the brickwork has any visual appeal. Then the masonry will probably have to be retuckpointed and damaged bricks will have to be replaced. Matching brick colors is always a frustrating ordeal. The best source of replacement brick is brickyards that salvage from demolition sites. Or check some demolition sites yourself. As a final option, the masonry can always be painted. If tastefully done, the building can be appealing, and it certainly will be more attractive than when covered by false siding.

A brick facade should conform to local traditions. Chicago's nineteenth-century architects and builders used two types of display brick — common and face brick. Face brick was usually red, although apartment buildings built after the turn of the century often have yellow or brown face brick. Facades made with face brick were generally laid with small mortar joints, an eighth of an inch or less, with the mortar flush to or raked back slightly from the surface. The mortar was white or an earth-tone red, brown or gray. When the mortar was colored white, it gave the wall fine but subtle lines, while a red or brown colored mortar blended into the wall, so that the facade appeared to be a solid mass. In either case mortar joints were not meant to be conspicuous or to clash with the bricks. Fortunately house owners with face brick facades have generally respected the building's integrity by maintaining the original color and the original shape of the mortar joints. The same has not been true with owners of common brick facades.

Common brick has a yellow clay-like color with a rough and non-shiny surface texture. Facades of common brick were generally laid with larger mortar joints than face brick facades, though mortar color was still chosen to blend with the brick. In the late Sixties, it became fashionable among some renovators to retuckpoint their common brick walls with a dark colored mortar, usually black or deep red, which high-lighted or emphasized each individual brick in the wall. In effect, the clashing mortar changes a brick wall into a wall of bricks. The eye no longer sees a solid mass; instead, each brick in the mass competes for the eye's attention. Visually, the dark clashing mortar joints make the wall look too active. A viewer does not know what he is supposed to focus on, and the building's original architectural ornaments are overwhelmed. Fortunately for the urban landscape, this fad seems to be waning.

If at all possible, a masonry facade, whether face or common brick, should be left unpainted. A painted wall is a solid mass or plane, albeit a colorful one, with a smooth texture. The paint covers both brick and mortar joint, destroying the fine lines of the contrasting mortar and obscuring the earth-tone of the brick. It mutes or obscures detail by making everything blend together. Many Victorian buildings of masonry construction were embellished with springcourses and decorative panels of terra cotta or glazed tiles. If these adornments are painted over, their visual appeal and charm are lost. Furthermore, to be practical, paint on a brick wall will wear and peel, as it does on a wood exterior; and if you are less than vigilant about maintaining the paint, the facade will soon appear piebald and unkempt. Of course if the brickwork is unattractive there is no alternative but to paint. Masonry was sometimes painted in the nineteenth century, and as long as it is done in tasteful, non-obtrusive colors such as white or light blue, yellow or gray, the painted exterior can be appealing.

Buildings with stone facades — granite, sandstone or limestone — have generally fared better over the years than their masonry or wood counterparts. This may be due not so much to the owner's reverence for the building as to the hardness of the stone. It is a major undertaking, after all, to knock a new window opening in a granite facade or to fill in a window opening with limestone. Consequently, most stone facades appear as they originally did, though a few have foolishly been covered with permastone. Buildings with stone facades may require some maintenance, but they need no improvement. Stone facades should be left unpainted. The mortar joints should be

Why would a person want to make the front of his house look like someone's backyard patio? The pink rocks on this old house have made it an eyesore conspicuous from a block away.

tuckpointed flush to the stone with mortar of neutral color, such as gray or earth-tone red.

WOOD-CLAD EXTERIORS

The wood-frame or balloon-frame house is Chicago's disdained and profaned offspring. No other type of building has suffered more disparagement. In areas of Chicago where wood-frame houses predominate, it is nearly impossible to find one with an original exterior. They have been covered with every material devised by man — asphalt sheets, asphalt shingles, masonite, false stone, false brick, vinyl and aluminum panels. It almost seems that a wood-frame building is an embarrassment. And yet the balloon-frame building is a Chicago invention.

The mother of this invention was the burgeoning population of nineteenth-century Chicago. When Chicago's tremendous population boom first started in the 1830s, wood-frame houses were still constructed by the Eastern brace frame method. In this method, the basic frame was made of hand-shaped heavy timbers, fitted together in elaborate joints fastened by wooden pegs. This slow and arduous building technique was totally inadequate to the housing needs of a rapidly expanding Chicago. A Chicago carpenter — most historians credit a man named Augustine D. Taylor — invented a simpler, faster construction method using stardard-sized milled studs and joists. The wood-frame houses that resulted from this new concept were so light, compared to their older counterparts, that the method was derisively nicknamed "balloon-frame."

Why Americans, especially Chicagoans, have so disdained the wood-clad wood-frame house is something of an enigma. It may have to do with the American perception of status — rich people can afford brick or stone, poor people can afford only wood. Thus people with wood-frame houses are forever trying to make them look like stone

The original charm of this wood-frame house becomes evident as its
disfiguring false siding is removed.

or masonry buildings. It is true that wood-clad houses must be painted periodically, yet many people with brick houses willingly subject themselves to the continuing responsibility of a painted exterior. And if there is a problem of esthetic disappointment with wood houses, it is self-inflicted and needless. Since most of these buildings were originally designed with pleasing proportions and attractive ornamentation, the way to make them appealing is obvious: restore the exterior to its original appearance.

The first step in restoring the exterior of a balloon-frame building is to remove the false siding. False siding may convey an impression of great solidity, perhaps because it is always promoted as "permanent," but you will find that it is easier to remove than you might expect, even in the case of permastone. The most common sidings, such as asphalt or masonite boards, are simply nailed over the clapboard. Pull out the nails and the siding comes off. If the nails have rusted, as they often do, the nail heads may break off, in which case you may have to use a hack-saw to cut the nails. Remove the false siding by starting at the bottom and working up. If the building is tall, a ladder may be dangerous and scaffolding should be considered.

Until the false siding has been removed, there is no way of knowing the condition of the underlying facade. The damage may be no greater than some cracks and holes made when the false siding was nailed on the clapboards. However, if moisture somehow got trapped under the false siding, the clapboard may have rotted. You might even find that for some reason the clapboards have been removed and the false siding applied directly to the wall sheathing.

Small holes and cracks in clapboard are no real problem — they can be filled with caulk. If the clapboards have warped and pulled away from the sheathing, you can screw them in place and then cover the screw heads with caulk. However, if the clapboards are rotted or badly fractured, they will have to be replaced (a clapboard with a single fracture can sometimes be repaired by screwing both sections firmly to the sheathing and filling the fracture crack with caulk).

However, it is possible that removing false siding will reveal a
badly damaged facade.

Replacing damaged clapboard is not difficult, nor does it require any special tools. A number of renovators in the Chicago area have replaced damaged clapboards on their houses themselves. The first step is to find replacement boards. Although clapboards have been known as clapboards for over a hundred years, some lumberyard employees claim ignorance of the term and use the words "beveled" or "lapped" siding instead. Clapboards are beveled or tapered so that the thicker part of one can overlap the thinner part of the next lower one.

Identifying the product is a minor nuisance; finding the right size is not. The standard clapboard widths in nineteenth-century Chicago were four inches and six inches. However, if you now ask for four-inch or six-inch clapboards at a lumberyard, you will get boards which actually measure only $3\frac{1}{2}$ or $5\frac{1}{2}$ inches wide. In addition, several renovators have bought the wrong size board by confusing the size of the board with the amount of board exposed or unlapped. Victorian builders were generally consistent in leaving four inches exposed from the bottom of one clapboard to the bottom of the next. This may seem like a four-inch clapboard, but the board's actual size is six inches, with two inches overlapped after installation. As a decorative effect, Victorian-era builders also used a smaller board with a $2\frac{1}{2}$-inch exposed area (the four-inch clapboard) usually just on the front facade. So when ordering replacement clapboard, do not forget that the board must be wide enough to accommodate overlapping. The modern narrower boards can be used to replace the original clapboard by allowing a little less overlap. On those few old houses that have a wide spacing (five inches or more) the six-inch replacement boards may be too small (since they are actually only $5\frac{1}{2}$ inches wide) in which case eight-inch boards may have to be used.

There are several "how-to" home repair books with good graphics and comprehensive instructions for replacing clapboards (see appendix). The key to the repair is in how the boards were nailed to the sheathing. There are two general methods — nails might pierce both boards at a point where they are overlapped, or the nails might fasten a single board. The former method is usually more difficult to deal with as there is the danger of damaging a good board nailed to the board being replaced. In such a case care must be taken, and nails may have to be cut rather than pulled out.

Before the new clapboards are nailed in place, they should be treated with a wood preservative, as any wood used outdoors should. Preservatives with penta-chlorophenol are generally very good. It would also be wise to paint the backside of the siding with a primer before nailing it in place. One unfortunate soul nailed on new wood siding without priming, and somehow water ran behind the clapboards and leached out natural coloring from the wood — it was probably redwood. This natural color seeped out and stained his new exterior paint. The clapboards had to be taken off, primed, reattached and repainted.

Because the purpose of removing false siding and restoring original clapboard is esthetic, only those areas of the exterior that are prominently visible from the street need to be restored. Balloon-frame houses in old neighborhoods on the North and Northwest Side were often built in a line with no more than three or four feet separating adjacent buildings. Since the sides and rear of such buildings are hardly visible, false siding that does require less maintenance might as well be left in place. However, if the false siding is to be removed from only the front facade, the corner boards should be uncovered as well. The corner boards are important visually as they define the form of the building. Six-inch redwood clapboard costs approximately 40 cents a linear foot. Clapboard to re-side an average-sized wooden facade will probably cost around $400, and of course many facades will not need to be re-sided completely.

ACCEPTABLE FALSE SIDING FOR WOOD HOUSES

Even though clapboard siding is relatively inexpensive and esthetically appealing, many building owners cannot resist the allure of "maintenance-fee" siding. Without question, wood siding commits you to repainting as old paint weathers away. However, false siding has disadvantages as well.

False siding is not really "maintenance-free." The exterior of any building will, with the passing of time, become soiled or stained. On some houses with false siding, the exterior has been unattended for so long that mold has actually begun growing in the built-up dirt. False siding should be cleaned about as often as clapboard should be painted. Nor does false siding always raise the value of the building, as siding salesmen often assert. On the contrary, if potential buyers find false siding unappealing (and this is more and more often true) the building's value may actually be reduced.

There are, however, some kinds of false siding which are appropriate for use on old clapboard houses. The newest sidings are made of aluminum, vinyl-coated aluminum and vinyl. Aluminum and vinyl siding come in two standard widths — eight inches and four inches. The four-inch design, called double-fours, is really a single panel eight inches wide, made to look like two four-inch boards. The eight-inch siding does not provide enough horizontal emphasis for tall, narrow balloon-frame houses. It is more appropriate for ranch-style suburban housing which is built with a horizontal emphasis to start with. As Victorian-era builders long ago discovered, horizontal lines spaced approximately four inches apart provide the most pleasing proportions for tall wood-frame houses. Only double-four siding should be used as a substitute for real clapboard siding.

Besides duplicating wood clapboard in size, false siding must also duplicate it in surface texture and appearance. Too many house owners believe that for something to look like wood it must have a surface texture with graining. Victorian-era builders, however, went to great lengths to achieve a smooth surface texture in their clap-boards. New vinyl siding with embossed graining not only fails to duplicate any known nineteenth-century siding, it does not even look like wood. Only double-four siding with a smooth texture and appearance is appropriate for old balloon-frame houses.

False siding must be chosen correctly, and then it must be applied with proper regard for the building's proportion and ornamentation. Vinyl and aluminum siding panels must be joined where they meet at the corners of the building. This can be achieved in either of two ways — by corner caps, or by corner post strips. Corner caps cover the joint where each row of panels meets at the corners. Corner post strips run the entire vertical length of the facade, covering all the corner joints at once. For old clapboard houses, corner post strips are by far the best choice because they provide vertical balance to the horizontal lines of the siding, just as the original corner boards did. Likewise the corner post strips should be the same width as the original corner boards; narrower strips will throw the building out of proportion.

Perhaps the most tragic consequence of the use of false siding has been that the beautiful original facade ornamentation of many wood frame houses — scroll work, cornices, decorative treatments around windows and doors — has been stripped off to make the installation of the siding cheaper and easier. This ornamentation should of course be preserved, even if this means that the exterior will not be completely "maintenance-free." A single afternoon's effort every five years to repaint the building trim is hardly a great exertion or expense. If the window or door trim is without appeal, then a casing of aluminum or vinyl does no harm. But the casing, as with the corner strips, should imitate traditional Victorian design. Generally, casing should be four or more inches wide, and it will provide the best effect if it is a contrasting color to the siding but the same color as the corner post strips.

Aluminum or vinyl double-four siding is not difficult to install, nor does it require any special tools. Nevertheless, the exterior of your house can be an embarrassing place to make a mistake. The trick to installing false siding is doing it so the siding is level and unwarped. The best place to purchase false siding is at a building supply outlet that caters to do-it-yourselfers by providing as much instruction and assistance as possible. At the very least, the outlet should provide free instruction manuals printed by siding manufacturers. The Architectural Aluminum Manufacturers Association (headquartered in Chicago) publishes an excellent application manual for distribution to outlet suppliers.

Vinyl double-four siding costs anywhere from $80 to $90 per square (100 square feet) which is in fact cheaper than wood clapboard. Generally, the cost to install false siding using a siding contractor is once and a half to twice the cost of doing it yourself. Whether a siding contractor is used or you choose to do it yourself, any old siding should be removed first.

WOOD ORNAMENTATION

If the original facade ornaments have been removed from your house, you may be able to locate replacements. Some wood ornaments, such as decorative brackets (corbels or consoles) are sold in salvage shops or by paint strippers as "architectural artifacts." The placement of missing ornaments can sometimes be discovered by following the outline of old paint, dirt and caulk that was left when the original ornaments were removed. Window cornices and trim, fretwork and sawnwood ornaments can usually be made by a good carpenter, millwork, cabinet maker or custom furniture maker at a reasonable cost. A simple decorative bracket costs about $30 and a stock window cornice about $20.

Fancy butt shingles are another Victorian wood adornment that at one time fell from favor, though they were usually covered with

Bargeboards, also called vergeboards or just verge, were a major part
of Victorian-era building ornamentation, but few have survived.

false siding rather than torn off. Butt shingles were cut in a variety of shapes — round, octagonal, fish-scale, pointed, hexagonal — and late nineteenth-century builders often used several different shapes, one row atop another, to make interesting patterns. (Houses with fancy butt shingles can be found in any old neighborhood, but the best areas in which to view them are Oak Park and Evanston, for old wood houses have fared better in these enlightened communities than in Chicago.) When false siding is removed, the butt shingles may be cracked, broken or rotted. Small nail holes can be repaired by filling with caulk, but broken, cracked or rotted shingles will have to be replaced.

Fancy butt shingles are still manufactured, but obtaining them often requires more effort than it should. *Shakertown Corporation* of Winlock, Washington, a major manufacturer of wood shingles, panels and shakes, still markets cedar fancy butt shingles. They come in nine shapes, both in the standard 16-inch length and 5-inch width for a 6-inch exposure, and in custom shapes or sizes. However, buying Shakertown's fancy butt shingles from a retail lumberyard is another matter. Most lumberyard employees have never heard of fancy butt shingles. Still, if the lumberyard distributes Shakertown products, then they can order fancy butt shingles. Unfortunately, many lumberyards demand large orders, such as two squares (enough shingle to cover two hundred square feet) and it often takes two months to get the shingles.

EXTERIOR RENOVATION OF AN
ILL-FAVORED WOOD HOUSE

Not every Victorian wood-frame house is a hidden beauty. Dozens of old balloon-frame houses amount to nothing more than a large box with five small window openings and a doorway. Removing the false siding from such a banal wood house cannot restore a beauty

When traditional design concepts are ignored in an exterior redesign
the result is a house out of balance or proportion.

that the house never had. These unattractive old wood houses are the dregs of the old house market, but they are not without advantages. They are often spacious inside, the address may be prestigious, and the houses may be relatively inexpensive.

The bane of the wood-frame house has always been the ease with which its facade can be redesigned. Masonry buildings were often victims of window redesign, but rarely was the entire facade completely reordered. Such work is too difficult and expensive to do with stone or masonry. Not so with wood. Redesigning or reconstructing the facade of a wood-frame house is a standard exercise in general carpentry — old siding and wall sheathing is removed, the old window openings are replaced with bearing studs, new openings are cut through old studs, and wall sheathing and siding is reinstalled. All of this may cost less than what the owner of a masonry building pays to save a badly deteriorated metal cornice. But in a sense, the bane of the wood-frame house is also its salvation. An unattractive wooden facade can be redesigned and reconstructed to become attractive.

However, redesigning the facade of any building must be done only with the greatest of caution and foresight. When the redesign of a wooden facade fails, the failure can almost always be traced to one of two mistakes. Either the vertical emphasis of a balloon-frame house has been ignored, resulting in poor proportion, or else the house has been made to look like something other than an old wood-frame house. To avoid these all-too-frequent mistakes, a facade should be reconstructed according to traditional Victorian design concepts. No one has yet provided a better method for dealing with the design problems of a tall, narrow building than the original Victorian designers.

Before embarking on actual alteration work, architectural drawings and perspectives of the new facade should be made. Since the reconstruction is bound to involve some work with load-bearing studs, an architect or structural engineer will have to submit drawings to the Building Department for a permit anyway, so he might as well be commissioned to do a perspective of the redesigned facade as well. How a building will look cannot be imagined satisfactorily without a picture, and the proposed design should be carefully worked out to provide the proper proportion, scale and balance.

To meet these goals the new facade must imitate Victorian materials as well as Victorian style. The proper siding for a Victorian wood-frame facade is four-inch clapboard, or as an acceptable substitute, smooth double-four vinyl or aluminum siding. However, under certain circumstances brick can be used. There is a certain degree of dishonesty in using brick on a wood house. Still, the basic architectural style — the tall, narrow house with a front-facing gable — was used just as often for masonry houses as for wood. And if the wood-frame building is built close to its neighbors and in a line, as they often were, then the sides of the building will not betray a false front. If the new brick facade is to appear Victorian in origin, however, the new masonry must be the same size, shape and color as Victorian masonry, with authentic Victorian mortar joints. One house owner on Bishop Street in the Near West Side put up a new facade using several different colors of brick. The facade is speckled in appearance, and, needless to say, it conflicts prominently with every other facade on the street. Another house owner on the Near Northwest Side installed a new facade of modern white glazed brick that evokes images of the interior of a hospital or the exterior of a White Castle hamburger stand. A new brick facade must blend, not conflict, with its Victorian neighbors. Using brick for a new facade will be more expensive than using clapboard, since a new support foundation will have to be excavated and poured in front of the main building foundation. The total cost to reconstruct a wood-frame facade will vary depending upon the size of the house, number of windows, and so on, but $5,000 is a reasonable estimate.

A banal wood-frame facade is made attractive by adhering to traditional Victorian concepts of design.

FENCES

One of the more melancholy trends in Chicago's redeveloping old neighborhoods is the proliferation of solid fences. Along many streets and boulevards of Chicago, the splendor and charm of Victorian houses is being obscured by large fences of brick and wood. As more and more solid fences are erected next to sidewalks, the pleasure of walking vanishes and the friendly and appealing ambience of a neighborhood is altered to one of hostility.

Fences around property lines, of course, are no recent innovation. Victorians often surrounded their property with seven-foot-high fences. However, the fences were iron, either cast or wrought, that did not obscure the street view of the house. Many mansions had cast-iron fences designed to match the building's roof cresting and railing posts. The need to restrict movement across property lines was easily met with simple iron picket fences.

Few Victorian fences, like so many things from the Victorian era, have endured. Ornate cast-iron and wrought-iron fences fell victim to a more noble purpose — patriotism and national survival. During World War II and to a lesser extent World War I, scrap iron drives were conducted to obtain scarce metal for the war effort. Citizens were asked to turn in all iron objects that were not absolutely necessary. Thus many of Chicago's original iron fences, gate posts, railings, and railing newel posts were sacrificed for the greater national cause. It was a matter of plowshares into swords.

Unfortunately, with the end of war few swords were forged or cast back into fences. Lost fences were replaced with cheaper chain-link cyclone fences or wood-picket fences. As a result, in 1946 the Chicago foundry that had cast most of the original newel posts and gate posts for Victorian houses went out of business. The owner of the foundry could not even interest anyone in buying the molds and patterns in case demand later revived. Old house owners rarely used iron fences anymore. Then, in the 1960s and '70s, brick walls began proliferating throughout all of the old neighborhoods in Chicago.

In part, large fences in old neighborhoods represent a fear of crime, a need for security. However, few fences can deter a burglar from entering a house he intends to rob. As a defensive measure, a solid fence is actually counterproductive; it offers the criminal sanctuary while preventing friendly neighbors from watching the space behind the walls. Many crimes have been prevented by vigilant neighbors who alerted police to suspicious activity in their area. For this reason, police always warn building owners not to build fences or plant large hedges. Moreover, a solid fence offers a great opportunity for graffiti artists. Their messages are sometimes threatening and always demoralizing to the citizens of a neighborhood. In terms of security, solid fences do not make good neighbors.

If there is a reason for erecting a solid fence (and often it seems that there is no reason; people erect them simply because everybody else has) it is not security but privacy. Every human needs some privacy, but a person who needs so much privacy that he must enclose his entire property with a seven-foot wall of brick or wood does not belong in the city. A city, after all, is a place where many people live close together. A sense of community and personal security should not be sacrificed for the privacy gained by using large solid fences.

The dangers, both esthetic and social, of solid fences in old neighborhoods have not escaped Chicago's urban planners and administrators. The Department of Urban Renewal's own study, "A Preliminary Study/Preserving the Architectural Character of a Neighborhood," conducted before the Lincoln Park project, recommended that solid fences "should generally be removed and outlawed." The guidelines of the Commission on Chicago Historical and Architectural Landmarks are much less emphatic, stating only that solid fencing "is not appropriate to Mid-North front yards." Solid fencing is indeed not appropriate for the Lincoln Park area, yet it has been proliferating there in front of old houses and new developments. Even prominent Chicago architects, who should know better, have

When solid fences proliferate along sidewalks, the urban landscape becomes cluttered and unattractive.

installed long stretches of brick wall next to their front sidewalks, and nearly all new construction in the Lincoln Park area has included an encircling brick wall.

Where streets are free of solid fencing, the credit is generally due to the efforts of enlightened residents. When the McCormick townhouses were sold into private ownership, the new property owners agreed not to erect any large fences on their property through Title Deed covenants. When the Near West Side redevelopment was initiated, residents agreed to remove their fences through the persuasion of the local Urban Renewal director. The reward for such community sophistication is an environment that is open and uncluttered.

Before erecting any fence, you as property owner should ask yourself whether there is really a need for a fence at all. Residents in the few areas where fences are banned admit there is a drawback in marauding kids and dogs. But if children and dogs must be prevented from disrespecting property rights, there is still no need to erect a large solid fence. A small fence, or even a hedge, no more than three or four feet high will effectively impede all but the most determined interlopers.

If you do need a fence in front of your house, by far the best choice is a fence of ornamental iron. There are half a dozen or more ironsmiths in Chicago who fabricate new ornamental iron picket fences. These fences are not inexpensive, and the more ornate the fence design, the greater the cost. In one recent renovation a house owner found that duplicating one section of an extremely ornate original fence would cost $900 per foot. A simple seven-foot-tall iron picket fence forged by an ironsmith will usually cost $35 per foot. Smaller three- or four-foot fences are, of course, cheaper. Several companies that specialize in chain-link and wood fences also sell iron picket fences, often for less than $35 per foot. This fencing is factory-produced and has hollow rather than solid pickets. A hollow metal fence looks right for old neighborhoods, but it is structurally weak and easily dented.

A fence-free neighborhood looks friendly and attractive.

Tending to building appearance is often the most painful part of an old house renovation because it involves spending money for non-essential purposes. You have no choice about repairing a leaking roof or replacing a worn-out furnace; but does it make sense to repair a tile roof when asphalt roll is cheaper, or to repair a cornice when you could just tear it down? Until quite recently, the answer to these questions, more often than not, has been, no. Strictly utilitarian considerations dominated thinking about housing, and the decorative touches so beloved by Victorian era builders were thought to be simply an annoying maintenance expense, if not actually in bad taste. The culmination of this point of view is the suburban tract house, which is cheap to build, ruthlessly efficient in its use of space, easy to maintain — and which has all the esthetic appeal of a refrigerator. Suddenly, however, attitudes have changed. Older homes are in great demand, the more "authentic" the better, and restoration of the original design is a solid financial as well as esthetic investment.

A plain brick fence is bad enough, but when someone uses brick to express his creativity, the result is a conspicuous neighborhood eyesore.

Appendix One

MULTI-UNIT BUILDINGS

A growing trend in redeveloping neighborhoods is the renovation of small multi-unit buildings, usually 2-, 3-, or 4-flats, by owner-occupants. The advantage of a multi-unit building is that it "pays for itself." Rent from the extra units often covers both the monthly mortgage and rehabilitation loan payments. Further, a multi-unit building provides tax advantages that are unavailable to owners of single-family residences. As an income-producing property a multi-unit building can be treated as capital for tax purposes, permitting the owner to deduct part of the building's value as depreciation. (*Depreciation* is the loss of value due to age, deterioration and obsolescence. The depreciation allowance applies only to the building's rental value, not to the value of the land under the building or to the owner's living unit.)

Financial institutions and government programs generally do not distinguish between single-family houses and small apartment buildings, as long as they are occupied by the owner. For example, the Federal Government's 312 loan program and Chicago's Financial Assistance to Property Owners' grant program are open to owners

When an apartment is entered by a turret window, chances are the building has been illegally divided. A prospective buyer should find out how many apartments are legal under the Zoning Ordinance and Building Codes before purchase.

of buildings of four units or less. Savings and Loans usually consider owner-occupied apartment buildings a good risk, especially if the apartments have tenants. However, buying an old multi-unit building as an investment rather than as a home is considerably more difficult. Such buildings are ineligible for government assistance and financial institutions are reluctant to offer mortgages for their purchase, reasoning that an absentee owner may abandon his building if the neighborhood does not redevelop as he hopes. Consequently financing, if available at all, is quite expensive — terms are often 35% down with 15 years to repay.

Zoning is the paramount difference between buying an old house and buying a multi-unit building in Chicago. The present zoning ordinance, enacted in 1957, zoned many neighborhoods of multi-unit buildings for single-family dwellings only. In such neighborhoods an old multi-unit building can be renovated only if it is transformed into a single family dwelling. Several building owners have found that just to enclose a second-story porch requires a zoning variation, which is obtained by a City Council vote on the recommendation of the local alderman — an obvious encumbrance to any renovation. Before purchasing a multi-unit building, you should be sure that the Zoning Ordinance will allow its renovation.

You should also be sure that the building you have in mind is legally a multi-unit building before you buy it. Many older buildings, especially large houses, were divided into smaller living units illegally. Even when they were legally divided, construction methods or materials may no longer conform to the Building Codes. One individual discovered that the basement apartments in his building had no firewall separators. He had to spend $10,000 before he could use the building as an apartment building. As the cost to bring an illegal multi-unit building into conformance with the Building Codes is usually quite high, have an expert inspect the building before purchase if there is any doubt about Code violations.

Often buyers of multi-unit buildings in redeveloping neighborhoods over-estimate the rents they can collect, assuming that rents will completely defray the high cost of renovation. However, in neighborhoods where redevelopment is still in its infancy, tenants who can afford high rent are scarce. Too many owners of apartment buildings in areas like Uptown or East Humboldt Park have gone broke or watched their property be destroyed by undesirable tenants. Before committing your life savings to renovating a multi-unit building, you should be sure that some residents of the neighborhood can afford high rents or else be willing and able to charge lower rents until the neighborhood can attract higher-income renters.

Buyers of multi-unit buildings must also understand the complexities of tenant leases, because these can interfere with renovation plans. A tenant lease is not voided because building ownership changes, nor do leases always expire at the same time. You may have to wait until the last lease has expired (which could be a year or two) to renovate the building, or else renovate each unit as it is vacated, which is usually more difficult and expensive. Before purchasing a multi-unit building, you and your lawyer should be sure that tenant leases will not be a problem. In addition, you should be sure that any tenant security deposits or advance rents are accounted for in the Sale Contract. Otherwise you may find yourself liable to your new tenants for several hundred dollars.

Inspecting an old multi-unit building prior to purchase is similar in most respects to inspecting a single-family dwelling. Plumbing should be carefully checked. Frequently water pressure in third-floor apartments is weak due to sediment and scale in risers. The only way to correct this is to replace the pipes, an expensive repair. Also, fireplaces in each unit should be checked for draft. Even though all fireplaces may be connected to the same chimney, some fireplaces may draft while others do not if a flue in the chimney has collapsed.

As you inspect a multi-unit building, one of your highest priorities should be to find out whether heat and electricity are billed and distributed to individual tenants or to the owner. The former is decidedly preferable. When each living unit controls its own heat and electricity, you as owner have fewer responsibilities for the comfort of your tenants, and you will probably save money as well. Of course renters know when they are paying for heat and electricity in their rent, but many are not conservation-conscious unless they receive a monthly utility bill as a reminder. If utilities are metered and billed to you as owner, you have to absorb the discrepancy between what your tenants are using and what you estimated they would use when you set the rent. If utility costs rise precipitously, as they did during the winter of 1973-74, this discrepancy can be serious, and you cannot adjust for it until tenant leases expire. You would probably be better off buying a cheaper building whose service systems are in complete disrepair and will have to be replaced anyway than buying a more expensive building whose service systems are functional but meterd to the owner.

One last word on multi-unit buildings: if you want to own an elegant Victorian apartment but are not sold on the responsibilities of a landlord, you might consider buying a condominium. Condominium ownership is a form of real property ownership. Each purchaser acquires a fee simple title to a specific unit in the building and to a specified percentage of undivided interest in all other portions of the property. In neighborhoods where single-family houses are scarce and multi-unit buildings prohibitively expensive, such as East Lake View or East Hyde Park, a condominium may be a buyer's only choice for an older home.

As with any multi-unit building, when you inspect a condominium one of the first things you should look for is how the building's services are distributed. Buildings with central heating and electricity are generally bad risks because some unit owners inevitably feel that they are paying for other peoples' heat and electricity. Relationships between owners are usually more harmonious in condominiums where utilities are controlled by and billed to individual units.

Because condominium owners hold some property in common,

such as garages, lobbies, and hallways, special problems can arise in their purchase and sale. Before you buy a condominium, be sure that the lawyer who represents you is experienced in condominium law. Your lawyer should ascertain that your property and responsibilities are clearly defined in the condominium documents — usually a Declaration and Association by-laws — and incorporated into the Sale Contract. Otherwise you may find that you are excluded from areas you thought were held in common, such as parking lots or recreation facilities, or that you are responsible for repairs that you assumed would be taken care of by the Condominium Association.

You and your lawyer must also be certain that the Sale Contract provides adequate safeguards to you as the buyer. A standard Sale Contract for a single-family dwelling usually has a "risk of loss" provision that relieves the purchaser of his obligation to buy the building if it is damaged before the closing, but a condominium Sale Contract may have a risk of loss provision that is limited to the unit being purchased. If common property is damaged under such a provision and you have signed the Sale Contract, you may be required to purchase the unit and pay your share of the common property repair.

For your lawyer to represent you properly, he must be knowledgeable in efficient condominium management as well as in condominium law. The condominium documents and Sale Contract may be complete and legal and yet still hold pitfalls for the unwary. For example, condominium documents often specify that Association decisions are to be made by unanimous vote. This is legal but terribly inefficient, since on many issues the Association will not agree. On the other hand, if decisions can be made by too small a majority, one group of the Association may gain too much control. This can be especially troublesome in cases of First Refusal. If a Condominium Association finds a potential buyer undesirable, they can exercise their Right of First Refusal and purchase the unit themselves, paying the seller what the potential buyer had offered for the unit. If too few votes are required to approve or reject a potential buyer, a small percentage of the Association may continually force the general membership to purchase units that have been offered for sale.

Locating a responsible attorney who is both experienced in condominium law and knowledgeable in condominium management is not always easy. Condominium law is, after all, only two decades old. The Chicago Bar Association will refer a specialist in condominium law upon request, although their referral list is limited to downtown lawyers. Community groups whose members live in condominiums may provide a more convenient source of referrals. For example, the Hyde Park-Kenwood Community Conference has an affiliate organization of condominium owners that maintains a referral list.

If you know so little about condominiums that just talking to a real estate agent or lawyer befuddles you, perhaps you should read the *Handbook on Illinois Condominiums* of the Illinois Institute for Continuing Legal Education. The Handbook was written for lawyers, but it is clear enough so laymen can gain much useful information. The Handbook is available at 29 S. LaSalle, 2nd floor, for $47.25. Or it can be read in the Cook County Law Library in the Civic Center Building (open to the public on weekdays to 9:00 pm).

Appendix Two

ADDITIONAL SOURCES OF INFORMATION

Buying and renovating an old house can be one of life's most exhilarating experiences. It can also be a morale-shattering nightmare. Preparation beforehand is the best guarantee of a good experience, so read as much as you can about house restoration, attend seminars or classes on the subject, tour restored houses and talk to as many experienced renovators as you can find — before you buy. This appendix describes the books, classes, tours and organizations most likely to benefit potential renovators in the Chicago area.

1. BOOKS

The *Complete Do-It-Yourself Manual* published by *Reader's Digest,* available at bookstores for $17, is probably the best of the dozens of home repair and remodeling guide books. It is comprehensive, lucid, and well-illustrated, and it covers more old house repairs, such as fixing a slate roof, than most books of the genre.

Remodeling Old Houses, by George Stephen (Knopf, $4.95) is
an excellent guide to the design and esthetic of old houses — a subject too often ignored by other writers. Stephen provides a lucid ex-
planation of proportion, scale and balance and writes in detail about
how to remodel or renovate an old house without destroying it. If
you must undo the ill-considered remodeling efforts of a previous
owner, this will be an important book for you.

Buying and Renovating a House in the City, by Deirde Stanforth
and Martha Stamm (Knopf, $5.95) provides an overview of the ren-
ovation experience and a survey of old house renovation across
America. The book is well-written and interesting but the authors
do not deal with specific repair or renovation techniques.

The Old House Journal, published monthly in New York City,
is the magazine of the old house renovation field. It provides the most
comprehensive and detailed instructions available on specific renovation techniques; people who have completed their own building
renovations often subscribe to it just to see what other people across
the nation are doing with their old houses. A typical issue will feature one specific old house restoration, several repair techniques, such
as plaster repair, fireplace rebuilding, masonry cleaning or wood refinishing, and an article on Victorian interior decoration — wall-
paper, drapes, and so on.

All the back issues of *The Old House Journal* are available
(it began in 1973) and the complete series amounts to the most detailed guide to old house renovation you can find anywhere. If you
read six years of *The Old House Journal,* you should never be a victim of a snow job or of the equivocations of contractors and tradesmen. *The Old House Journal* is available for $12 annual subscription
from 199 Berkeley Place, Brooklyn, New York 11217.

2. COURSES

There are several places in Chicago that offer classroom or workshop
instruction on old house renovation. These seminars are valuable not

only for the information they render but also as a means of meeting people who are knowledgeable about old house renovation in the Chicago area. The instructors are generally professionals or experienced renovators, and they often know of skilled artisans who can perform difficult repairs. Furthermore, people enrolled in the course may have useful information on repair techniques, artisans, contractors, and so on.

The Landmark Preservation Council at 407 S. Dearborn, Chicago (the Old Colony Building) 922-1742, offers a seminar on old house renovation that covers such subjects as evaluating the condition of a building, exterior maintenance, restoring the charm and character of the house, financial and legal aspects, and understanding basic building service systems. The course is conducted by various professionals involved in building renovation. LPC usually presents their old house renovation course on Saturdays in the spring. The cost in the past has been around $35 to $40.

The Landmark Preservation Council also often presents seminars on building renovation in conjunction with other institutions and organizations. In the past seminars were given in Wilmette cosponsored by the Wilmette Historical Society, in the Chicago Cultural Center cosponsored by the Chicago Public Library and in the Chicago Historical Society cosponsored by the Chicago Department of Planning. These seminars are irregularly scheduled, so you will have to ask LPC if any are planned.

Francis Parker School, a private school at 330 West Webster, Chicago, conducts an evening adult education program with several courses targeted to people renovating an old house. *Recycling Old Buildings* is a practical course covering such topics as Code compliance, permit procedures, financing and repair techniques. A tour of various rehabilitated buildings is usually included as part of the course. Besides the *Recycling* course, there are several decorating and remodeling courses that may also be of interest: *Do-It-Yourself Decorating, Electrical Home Repair,* and *Kitchen and Bathroom Design and Remodeling.* Francis Parker courses usually last six weeks, cost $40 and are offered in the spring and fall.

The Latin School, another private school, at 59 West North Avenue, Chicago, also offers evening adult education courses. However, the Latin School's curriculum is not as oriented towards practical self-repair as Francis Parker's. (The Latin School mainly serves Chicago's Gold Coast, where renovations are conducted by architects and interior designers.) Still the Latin School does offer some decorating courses that include aspects of renovation. Latin School courses cost $40 and are offered in the spring and fall.

Another organization that presents seminars and lectures of some relevance to old house renovation is the *ArchiCenter.* The Archi-Center, at 310 South Michigan, Chicago, 2nd floor, is actually an exhibition center instituted as a Bicentennial project and now administered by the Chicago Architecture Foundation. The ArchiCenter presents a continuing series of lectures on subjects pertinent to architecture and preservation. One month the subject may be recycling old buildings, the next, landscaping or preservation in historic districts. Most lectures are presented at noon and some in the late afternoon, and all are free. Besides lectures, the ArchiCenter has exhibits, slide shows and a small bookstore limited to architecture, preservation and renovation.

City House — There are presentations on various aspects of building renovation at the annual City House trade show held in the spring at Navy Pier. Sponsored by the National Trust for Historic Preservation and the Commission on Chicago Historical and Architectural Landmarks, City House is a "home improvement exposition of products and services suited to the rehabilitation of older Chicago-area houses." The show does present much useful information, but with thousands of people crowded together, it is difficult receiving that information.

In addition to classroom presentations on the subject of building renovation, craft shop courses on woodworking can sometimes be useful to those attempting general carpentry repair in their old houses. Several people with little prior experience in woodworking were able to duplicate missing wood ornamental trim by completing a woodworking course. The Chicago Park District conducts a city-wide craft program with a heavy stress on woodworking. There are over 50 Park District field houses dispersed throughout Chicago with wood shops and craft instruction. The cost to use Chicago Park District shop facilities is five dollars per year. (For information call 294-2323 or any individual field house.)

3. COMMUNITY ORGANIZATIONS

The fastest way to meet people who have renovated or are renovating an old house is through community organizations in old neighborhoods. Some organizations maintain a list of recommended contractors and artisans. If they do not, individual members of the organization usually have such information. If you are moving into a blighted or depressed neighborhood, joining the local community organization is a matter of self-interest and defense. It is only through collective action that a neighborhood turns from deterioration to regeneration.

The Lincoln Park Conservation Association, at 746 W. Fullerton, Chicago (477-5100), maintains an up-to-date reference file on contractors, artisans, handymen, etc. In addition, LPCA has a schedule of events, activities and meetings of its several affiliated neighborhood organizations. LPCA's artisan reference file was assembled for the benefit of its membership and their policy is to require people to pay a membership fee to use the contractor reference file. In all fairness, anyone using the services of a community organization should pay for it since most community groups exist on shoe-string budgets. Nevertheless, in the past LPCA has given out contractor references without demanding a membership fee.

The Hyde Park-Kenwood Community Conference, at 1400 East 53rd Street, Chicago is the South Side equivalent to the North Side Lincoln Park Conservation Association. The Hyde Park-Kenwood Community Conference also has a reference list of contractors and tradesmen maintained by the South Side Condominium Co-Op Owners Association, an affiliate of the Hyde Park-Kenwood Community Conference, which they will sell to non-members for $5.

The Old Wicker Park Committee, at 1527 N. Wicker Park Avenue (342-1966) is a relatively new community organization attempting to marshall the redevelopment of their beset West Town neighborhood. OWPC usually meets the first Monday of each month at St. Paul's Evangelical Lutheran Church at 2215 W. North Avenue, and they welcome visitors to their monthly meetings so they can promote the virtues of their neighborhood. The OWPC has also begun a contractor reference file, which, at present, they are willing to share with non-members.

The Logan Square Neighborhood Association, at 2641 North Milwaukee Avenue, Chicago is an established community organization formed years ago to arrest neighborhood blight. LSNA never bothered to assemble a contractor-tradesmen reference list; however, the organization itself has purchased and renovated several abandoned old buildings in the area and thus has some first-hand knowledge about local contractors.

The Lake View Citizens Council, at 3245 North Sheffield, Chicago, is an umbrella organization encompassing dozens of smaller neighborhood organizations, block clubs and church groups. The Lake View Citizens Council never assembled a contractor-tradesmen reference list because, until recently, there was no building renovation in the area more extensive than a house owner covering his building with false siding. Nevertheless, anyone buying an old house in the Lake View area should consider joining the Lake View Citizens Council as it has been very successful at effecting beneficial neighborhood change. LVCC was responsible for the down-zoning of Eastern Lake View, controlling the proliferation of high-rises in the area, and prohibiting cheap jerry-built apartment buildings known as four plus one's. Furthermore, since most people in Lake View who have renovated an old house have joined LVCC or one of the smaller affiliated neighborhood groups, joining the organization is a way to meet people with helpful information to impart.

The Pullman Civic Organization, at 614 East 113th Street (the Hotel Florence), Chicago, is a testimony to the value of community action and organization. In the early 1960s the City of Chicago had recommended that Pullman be demolished for industrial redevelopment. Rather than accept extinction, Pullman residents formed a community organization, the Pullman Civic Organization, and resolved to save their community. Ten years later Pullman became a Chicago and national landmark district. The Pullman Organization and its offshoot, the Historic Pullman Foundation, is still orchestrating the restoration and preservation of Pullman today. The Historic Pullman Foundation has most of the original architectural drawings of residential buildings in the area and samples of original paints and wallpapers used in Victorian Pullman.

The Housing Center, at 2321 E. 71st (363-4545), is a newly formed organization that serves as a clearing house of information for people in the South Shore area. The Housing Center maintains current information on government programs, tenant co-ops, condominium regulations, etc. They are also starting a contractor reference file. Until a list of their own is assembled, they are using the Department of Planning's list of certified contractors.

4. TOURS

If you are completely unfamiliar with house renovation, one pleasant and useful way to garner information is to tour previously renovated old houses. Tours can provide leads on architects, contractors, and

artisans, and they can help you to decide what kind of interior renovation you prefer. Community organizations and foundations often
sponsor tours of renovated houses for fundraising and publicity, and
neighbors or acquaintances who have renovated their homes are generally receptive to interested visitors.

The Glessner House, at 18th and Prairie Avenue, Chicago (326-
1393) is a landmark house being restored by the Chicago Architecture Foundation. The Glessner House will be the focal point of the
Prairie Avenue Historical District, a historical restoration being conducted by the City of Chicago which will eventually include the oldest building in Chicago, the Henry Clarke House. Before the Chicago
Architecture Foundation began working on the Glessner House in
1967, the building had been used — or abused — by a printing firm.
Woodwork had been painted, staircase balusters were missing, fireplace tiles were broken, and in general the problems facing the Chicago Architecture Foundation were similar to those of individuals
renovating an old house. The Glessner House can be toured on weekends and on Tuesdays and Thursdays. The cost is $2.

The Chicago Architecture Foundation's subsidiary organization,
the *ArchiCenter,* also sponsors a tour of restored mansions in historical districts, usually during the summer.

In Oak Park, the *Frank Lloyd Wright Home and Studio Foundation* is restoring Frank Lloyd Wright's original house and studio, at
Chicago and Forest Avenues, Oak Park (848-1978). The Foundation
also runs the *Oak Park Tour Center,* which conducts tours of the
Oak Park Historic District. The Wright home can be toured on Tuesdays, Thursdays and weekends. The Farson Mills House, which
houses the Museum Room of the Historical Society of Oak Park and
River Forest, can also be toured.

One of the largest restoration projects in the Chicago area is the

Naper Settlement in suburban Naperville. Under the auspices of the Naperville Heritage Society, nine old buildings are being restored as a nineteenth century village. The project has entailed such difficult work as moving several old buildings from one site to another. Besides Naper Settlement, the Naperville Park District has for many years maintained the *Martin-Mitchell House* (EL5-0274) a large and ornate Victorian mansion, as a museum of the Victorian way of life. Naper Settlement and the Martin-Mitchell House are located on Aurora Avenue (Route 65) just west of the central business district. It can be toured on Wednesdays and Sundays, 1:30 to 3:30 pm.

Most publicly maintained Victorian houses are either international landmarks, like the Wright house, or luxuriant mansions, like the Charles Gates Dawes Mansion in Evanston. Neither of these is typical of the old houses most people buy and renovate. More representative of the Victorian home is the *Frances Willard House* at 1730 Chicago Avenue, Evanston. Lovingly preserved by the Women's Christian Temperance Union. Willard House is open for tours on week days or by arrangement with the WCTU hostess.

Several suburban historical societies are housed in restored or preserved Victorian houses. *The Lombard Historical Museum,* at 23 West Maple Street, Lombard, is a frame house of the 1870s maintained in the style of the period. *The Evanston Historical Society* is quartered in the Charles Gates Dawes Mansion at 225 Greenwood Street, Evanston, and the *Elmhurst Historical Museum* is housed in the Glas Mansion, at 104 South Kenilworth Avenue. The *Aurora Historical Museum* at Oak and Cedar, Aurora is a 20-room mansion built in 1856. The *Downers Grove Park District* maintains a historical museum in a Victorian frame house, the Wandschneider House, on Maple Avenue. If nothing else, touring these preserved Victorian houses will give you a good idea of whether you like Victorian furniture and interior decoration or whether you should opt for a more contemporary interior decor instead.

In addition to touring institutionally maintained old houses, you can participate in various house tours sponsored by community organizations. *The Historic Pullman Foundation,* at 614 East 113th Street, Chicago (785-8181), usually sponsors an annual tour of several Pullman houses ranging from faithful restorations to more modern renovations. The Pullman tour in the past has been conducted in early October. *The Latin School* and *Francis Parker School* both sponsor house tours, usually in late spring, around the theme of "city living." Usually twelve houses of diverse styles, from restored mansions with period furniture to contemporary renovated houses to new Newberry Plaza townhouses are toured. The Francis Parker tour in the past has been a single day weekend affair, costing $10, while the Latin School tour has been a regularly scheduled evening adult education course, at regular tuition cost with two houses toured each session.

The Mid-North Association (an LPCA affiliate) in 1978 began sponsoring a house tour of renovated houses as a fund-raising project. The tour of eight landmark houses for $10 is one of the city's best.

The Beverly Area Planning Association, in the Beverly Art Center, 2153 W. 111th Street, sponsors a house tour of the Beverly-Morgan Park area, usually in the spring.

Although *Galena* may be a half day's drive from Chicago, for those few people in the Chicago area renovating a house built prior to 1871, Galena is a good place to seek information. In the early Victorian decades, 1830s and 1840s, while Chicago was still trying to extract itself from lakefront mire, Galena was a prosperous, growing Midwestern city graced with many fine and ornate mansions. However, when the lead mines of Galena were exhausted in the post-Civil War years, the city went into a protracted decline. After a century of neglect, Galena has been "discovered" and redeveloped by young couples in much the same manner as Lincoln Park and Wicker Park in Chicago. In June of each year, the Galena Historical Society sponsors a tour of five restored Galena mansions. In addition, the Ulysses S. Grant home is now a completely restored museum and several hotel-inns and antique shops are landmark-class buildings open to public view.

Another Illinois village worth visiting for information about restoration of early Victorian houses is *Bishop Hill*. Bishop Hill, about one hundred and sixty miles from Chicago near Kewanee, was an offspring of the religious utopian movement of the early nineteenth century. Built by Swedish immigrants in the 1840s through 1860s, Bishop Hill suffered the fate of most utopian experiments. Bishop Hill became just another Illinois village after the religious founder of the colony was shot and killed by his son-in-law. After a century of decay and neglect, Bishop Hill is now being restored by the State of Illinois, various private preservation groups and some descendants of the original immigrants.